Robert E Preston

History of the monetary legislation and of the currency system of the United States

Embracing rare and invaluable documents

Robert E Preston

History of the monetary legislation and of the currency system of the United States

Embracing rare and invaluable documents

ISBN/EAN: 9783741186301

Manufactured in Europe, USA, Canada, Australia, Japa

Cover: Foto ©Thomas Meinert / pixelio.de

Manufactured and distributed by brebook publishing software (www.brebook.com)

Robert E Preston

History of the monetary legislation and of the currency system of the United States

"Thy silver is become dross."—Isaiah i. 22.

HISTORY

OF THE

MONETARY LEGISLATION

AND OF THE

CURRENCY SYSTEM OF THE UNITED STATES.

EMBRACING

RARE AND INVALUABLE DOCUMENTS.

By HON. ROBERT E. PRESTON,
DIRECTOR OF THE MINT.

TO WHICH IS ADDED A SPEECH

ON

OUR CURRENCY SYSTEM.

By HON. JAMES H. ECKELS,
COMPTROLLER OF THE CURRENCY.

JOHN J. McVEY,
PHILADELPHIA.
1896.

COPYRIGHT
1896
BY JOHN J. MCVEY.

PREFACE.

"WHEN the mariner has been tossed for many days in thick weather and on an unknown sea, he naturally avails himself of the first pause in the storm, the earliest glance of the sun, to take his latitude and ascertain how far the elements have driven him from his course."* Not for a few days only, nor for a few months, nor even for a few years, but for twenty, have the monetary pilots of the United States, entrusted with the care of the ship of state, been tossed about upon the waters, by the jarring winds of false financial doctrines; yet so far from availing themselves of the pauses in the storm that have occasionally given them a glimpse of the sun and light to determine their bearings and position, and discover how far they had drifted or been driven from the course of the correct principles of currency legislation, they seem bent rather on steering clear of the right path and sailing, without chart or compass, one knows not whither, except that it must be through darkness to danger and, perhaps, disaster.

One such glimpse they had after the clouds of the crisis of 1893 began to clear away. Others have come to them after the successive issues of bonds during the past two years, resulting in the borrowing of $250,000,000 to maintain a reserve of $100,000,000, which is ever oozing out of the Treasury, and which cannot be kept intact so long as the Treasury-draining tubes of the legal-tender notes and Treasury notes are not stopped up or destroyed—a reserve which must be replenished periodically to insure the parity with

---

* From Webster's Reply to Hayne.

gold of our paper money amounting to over $800,000,000, and to avert the "circulating pest"* of a depreciated medium of exchange. But neither the light after the panic nor after the ever-recurring embarrassments of the Treasury, followed by repeated and heavy loans, in a time of profound peace, has sufficed to let them see that the panic was produced and the issues of bonds rendered necessary by the fact that they had been violating, for over twenty years, every law of coinage and finance, and that the proper preventative of such panics and bond issues in the future is to ascertain how far they have been driven from the true course of monetary principles—of the principles that have guided all other great commercial nations since 1871, and that had directed the monetary legislation of the United States for nearly ninety years—the monetary principles of the Fathers of the Republic, of Robert Morris, Thomas Jefferson, and Alexander Hamilton.

The article here reprinted from the Report of the Director of the Mint, 1895, on the Monetary Legislation and Currency System of the United States, embodying as it does such rare and invaluable documents as those of Robert Morris, Superintendent of Finance: On a Coinage Scheme for the United States (1782), of Thomas Jefferson: On the Establishment of a Money Unit (1782 or 1783), of Alexander Hamilton: On the Establishment of a Mint (1791)†, and of the Hon. John Sherman on the part that should now be played by silver in our currency (1877), are the best possible antidotes that can be administered to neutralize the virus of the monetary heresies that has been absorbed by a large part of the voting population of the United States. The keen and subtle analysis of the Report of Alexander Hamilton on the Establishment of a Mint by the Hon. Robert

---

* The first Napoleon thus described a depreciated, inconvertible paper currency, but the words are equally applicable to a metallic depreciated currency.

† Hamilton's Report on the Establishment of a Mint can be found nowhere except in his complete works in 9 volumes which cost about $100, and in the Report of the International Monetary Conference of 1878, now out of print and almost unobtainable.

E. Preston, the present Director of the Mint, will be read with interest and profit by all who desire to learn what were the currency principles of our forefathers and to be guided by them, as will also what Mr. Preston has to say on currency reform, and the free coinage of silver, whether they be Democrats or Republicans—for the currency question is not one of party, but of business integrity. Morris, Jefferson and Hamilton were honest, well-intentioned men, addressing themselves to other honest and well-intentioned men, desirous of the truth.

This pamphlet is issued in behalf of no political party, but solely as a contribution to the cause of a sound and stable currency, in which all American citizens, rich and poor alike, are interested—many much more vitally than they are themselves conscious of.

Mr. Preston's article is followed by one on a cognate subsubject by the Hon. James H. Eckels, Comptroller of the Currency, whose judicious administration of his important office contributed more than any other single agency to mitigate the hardships of the crisis of 1893, and whose distinguished services in that behalf will be long held in remembrance by a grateful people.

Whether such was their intention or not, Morris, Jefferson and Hamilton followed, in the matter of the coinage, the Biblical injunctions:

Ye shall do no unrighteousness in judgment, in meteyard, in weight, or in measure.
Just balances, just weights, a just ephah, a just hin, shall ye have.
Leviticus xix. 35, 36.
Thou shalt not have in thy bag divers weights, a great and a small.*
Thou shalt not have in thy house divers measures, a great and a small.
But thou shalt have a perfect and just weight, a perfect and just measure shalt thou have. *Deuteronomy xxv. 13, 14, 15.*
Shall I count them pure with the wicked balances, and with the bag of deceitful weights? *Micah vi. 11.*

---

* The ancient Hebrews effected their exchanges by means of *pieces* of silver, and carried in a bag a balance and weights to determine the quantity of the precious metal to be parted with in case of a purchase, or received in case of a sale. *Genesis xx. 16; xxxvii. 28; xlii. 27, 35; xlv. 22.*

The best proof that Morris, Jefferson and Hamilton were, consciously or unconsciously, imbued with these Scriptural precepts, is to be found in the following utterances of these distinguished men to be found in their published writings:

"The Secretary is upon the whole strongly inclined to the opinion that a preference ought to be given to neither of the metals for the money unit. * * * Perhaps if either were to be preferred it ought to be gold rather than silver. * * * The inducement to such a preference is to render the unit as little variable as possible, because on this depends the steady value of all contracts, and in a certain sense of all other property. * * * But upon the whole, it seems to be most advisable not to attach the unit exclusively to either of the metals; because this cannot be done effectually without destroying the character of one of them as money and reducing it to the situation of a mere merchandise. * * * * There can hardly be a better rule in any country for the legal than the market ratio. * * * * The chief inducement to the establishment of the small gold piece is to have a sensible object in that metal as well as in silver to express the unit."—*Alexander Hamilton.*

"I concur with you that the unit must stand on both metals."—*Thomas Jefferson.*

"Just principles will lead us to disregard legal proportions altogether, and to inquire into the market price of gold and silver in the several countries, with which we shall be principally connected in commerce, and to take an average from them."—*Thomas Jefferson.*

"There is a great impropriety not to say injustice in compelling a man to receive a part of his debt in discharge of the whole."—*Robert Morris.*

"Arguments are unnecessary to show that the scale by which everything is to be measured ought to be as fixed as the nature of things permit of.—*Robert Morris.*

In the language of the present day, in their bearing on our currency system, or our money, the verses cited above from Leviticus, Deuteronomy, and Micah, would read something like this:

Thou shalt not have in thy purse divers dollars, a gold one of one hundred cents and a silver one of fifty cents, metallic value.

But thou shalt have a perfect and just dollar, a gold one of 23.22 grains, and a silver one of 743.04 grains (the weight a silver dollar would have at the ratio of 1 : 32, nearly the actual market ratio in 1895), a perfect and just measure of value shalt thou have.

Shall I count them pure, with the wicked fifty-cent dollars, and with the purse of deceitful measures of value?

The principles above laid down by Morris, Jefferson and

Hamilton, were, as Hon. Robert E. Preston shows, respected in every coinage act of the United States up to the passage of the Bland act in 1878, when every one of them was disregarded. They were followed in the coinage acts of 1792, 1834, 1837, 1853, and 1873. The full legal tender silver coins minted under all these acts were honest dollars, for they contained, as nearly as possible, pure silver worth a dollar in gold, so that when melted down the bullion obtained from them could be sold for a gold dollar. At the present time, a silver dollar, when melted down, cannot be sold for over fifty cents in gold. What becomes of the other half of its value? It was not in the silver dollar, and the government imprint testifying that it was worth a dollar (gold being still the unit of value) or 23.22 grains of pure gold, was, in plain Anglo-Saxon, a lie.

Our present silver coinage violates the principles of morality, since it compels a man to receive part of his debt in discharge of the whole. The creditor to whom a dollar is due is entitled to 23.22 grains of pure gold or to its equivalent in something else. Now the owners of silver mines in the West exchanged for 23.22 grains of pure gold in 1895, an average weight of pure silver of 743.04 grains. The silver dollar contains only 371¼ grains, or 371¾ less than it should.

Our silver coinage violates the principles of metallic currency of Morris, Jefferson and Hamilton, also in this: that the ratio in the coinage is not the commercial ratio.

Indeed, as any one who carefully reads Mr. Preston's paper will see, if he is acquainted with the monetary systems of other countries, the currency system of the United States is the worst, the most illogical, the most inconsistent, the most dangerous, and most expensive, the most unscientific and unstatesmanlike, possessed by any civilized nation since the beginning of this century. Its illogicalness, inconsistency, incoherency, and dangerousness, have been fully demonstrated by Mr. Preston; and it is only necessary to add here to what he has said a few words on its expensiveness.

In about two years the United States has borrowed, to maintain a gold reserve of $100,000,000, $250,000,000. Since 1879, the average amount of the reserve at the close of the fiscal year has been $137,941,582. The interest on this sum at 4 per cent. for 17 years is $93,800,271. The silver purchased under the Bland act and the Sherman act cost $464,210,262.96. At the average price of silver in 1895, viz., $0.6806 per ounce fine, that same silver was worth only $302,672,526.06. The loss by depreciation has been, therefore, $161,537,736.90. Up to March 13, 1896, the greenbacks fully redeemed since January 1, 1879, amounted to $386,000,000. As these $386,000,000 were reissued, they are in the nature of a new forced loan which must yet be paid, and, therefore, charged as part of the cost of our monetary system since 1879. The expenditure account, therefore stands thus:

Borrowed to maintain the reserve	$250,000,000
Interest on average reserve for 17 years	93,800,271
Depreciation of silver purchased under Bland and Sherman Acts	161,537,737
Legal tenders redeemed but re-issued	386,000,000
Total	$891,338,008

And this does not include interest on the loans made during the last two years to maintain the gold reserve.

In a few more years, if the same causes are allowed to operate, the cost of our monetary system since 1879 will be $1,000,000,000, or fully as much as the enormous sum France had to pay to Germany as an indemnity after the Franco-Prussian War of 1870–71, and considerably more than one-third of our national debt after the close of the war of secession, when (August 31, 1865) it amounted to $2,844,649,626.56—the highest figure it has ever reached. Leaving out of the account coin certificates and treasury notes offset by an equal amount of specie in the treasury, our national debt on December 31, 1895, was $1,125,325,462—a sum which the cost of our currency system will reach before the end of the next administration, unless it is reformed, or the country goes on the silver basis.

But our currency system is not only expensive, it is pregnant with danger to individuals and to the nation —to individuals, because it may at any time in the future, unless reformed on the lines laid down by Mr. Preston, and in accordance with the principles of coinage enunciated by Morris, Jefferson and Hamilton, lead to a crisis similar to that which occurred in 1893, from the effects of which the country is only now recovering—a crisis which would produce widespread commercial and financial ruin.

The silverites are still loud in their demands for free coinage of the white metal. It requires but very little thought to discover that while the producers of silver would be temporarily—but only temporarily—benefited by such a measure, all other classes, with the exception of dishonest debtors anxious to discharge their obligations by means of fifty-cent dollars, would be injured. The owners of silver mines would reap a profit if a free-coinage-of-silver act were passed, because they would receive for every ounce of silver minted a bonus of at least 60 cents.

The average price of silver per ounce fine in 1895 was very nearly 65½ cents. Coined an ounce would circulate at $1.2929, or $0.6379 more than it is worth. The difference would go into the pockets of the owners of silver mines. Is it any wonder that they favor free coinage at the ratio of 1 : 16 of the metal they produce? But this profit even to them would be only temporary. The increased and arbitrary price given to silver by legislation might result in at least a doubling of the production of the metal in the United States and elsewhere. The silver output of the United States in 1894 was nearly $64,000,000 (coining value). Under the stimulus of a profit of 100 per cent. it might soon rise to $130,000,000 in the United States alone. When we came to have an annual addition to our coinage of $130,000,000 under the operation of a free-coinage-of-silver law, the purchasing power of silver would drop to, perhaps, one quarter of what it is at present. Prices would rise, as they always do when the circulating medium becomes excessive, but the purchasing price of the silver dollars—which would then, in the form of silver certificates, constitute our sole medium of exchange—would not be over that of twenty-five cent pieces now. The prices of wheat, of cotton and tobacco, would increase; but the seller of wheat, cotton and tobacco would require four dollars then to purchase what he now obtains for one. Receivers of pensions or fixed salaries would be robbed of three-fourths of their income, since they would receive the same nominal amount, with a purchasing power of only one-fourth of their income at present. The man who had toiled and pinched himself during his whole life to leave the mother of his little ones an insurance of say $5,000 or $10,000, would really leave them only the equivalent of $1,250 or $2,000 of our present money. It should never be forgotten that the only classes who could be benefited by the passage of a free coinage bill would be the owners of silver mines and dishonest debtors. All others, and wage earners and wage-workers principally, would suffer; for the working classes are always the last whose remuneration is increased when, in consequence of the inflation of the currency, there is a general rise of prices—a rise of rents, of articles of clothing, of fuel, of tea, and coffee, of beef, and butter, and bread. Let the workmen think of this, and not imagine that the only persons interested in an honest dollar are bankers, and brokers, and presidents of railway companies. An honest dollar is of greater value relatively to the poor than to the rich. Payment made in dishonest dollars may mean a loss to the rich man—a loss he can bear without impoverishment, perhaps. To the poor man it may mean starvation—a lack of food, of clothing and of shelter.

Nor can the Nation be insensible to the evils of a depreciated silver currency. When it was seen recently that there was a possibility of our becoming involved in a war with England, our prospective foe on the other side of the Atlantic found great comfort in the thought that, to carry on such a war, we should have to borrow gold in Europe, especially in London, the great money market of the world, and that London would not let us have it. Had we the gold standard, we should have an abundance of international money, and no such threat could have been made. Our present currency system, viewed from a military standpoint, is an element of weakness; and patriotism no less than morality, business foresight, and financial wisdom calls loudly for its reform.

Our legislators have by Act of Congress clipped or sweated out of every silver dollar a quantity of pure metal valued at 50 cents. If an individual citizen, in his private capacity, had clipped out a much smaller portion of the dollar, he would, under Section 5459 of the Revised Statutes, have rendered himself guilty of a crime and liable to a penalty of not more than two years imprisonment at hard labor and a fine of not less than $2000—of a crime the punishment for which in England, in the last century, was that the culprit should be hanged by the neck until he was dead. The punishment was severe; but it must be remembered that the crime was a grievous one, for the issuer of false coin, the debaser of the coinage, is not only a robber himself, but makes every man who knowingly or innocently passes the coin he has debased a robber in turn, thus multiplying his own wrong a hundred or a thousand, perhaps ten thousand times.

One of the most alarming symptoms of our public life is that such legislative crimes as that of the debasement of the coinage by Act of Congress are viewed not only with unconcern at the enormity perpetrated but even with approval by so many of our public men and by so large body of voters. Well does Mr. Preston say:

"During the last generation—that is, ever since the 25th of February, 1862, when the Government of the United States made its paper evidences of indebtedness legal tender—many have naturally grown up with all sorts of misconceptions and delusions on the important subject of the currency. Hence it is that their fundamental notion of money is a false one, and although they know full well that the silver coins of the United States at present owe nearly half their value to the stamp of the mint which they bear and the pledge of the Government to maintain them at par with gold, and that, to that extent, the value of these silver coins is fictitious and not real, they persist in preferring shadow to substance in the currency of the country, or at least to consider shadow quite as good as substance. Although aware that 1,000 silver dollars bearing the stamp of the United States mint, thrown into the melting pot and reduced to the form of bullion, will produce a quantity of metal that will yield the holder little more $500 in any market of the world, while 1,000 gold dollars also bearing the stamp of the United States, subjected to the same process, will come out of the crucible still worth $1,000 in any country of the world, they insist that the silver and the gold are equally good currency.

They have apparently never asked themselves what becomes of nearly 50 per cent. of the value of the silver dollar after the stamp of the United States mint has been obliterated from it and it has been changed in shape; in what the departed value consisted while the stamp remained intact and the form of the coin unaltered; whether the lost value was real or imaginary; whether the stamp was the expression of a truth or the contrary; and whether, without the whole power of the courts and of the executive back of it, the silver dollar would pass on its own intrinsic merits, or otherwise than by the compulsory circulation given it by the strong hand of the law. If, indeed, the law favored neither a gold currency above a silver currency, nor a silver currency above a gold, but left it to the free and unconstrained action of the citizens to choose between them, they would invariably choose that which was always and everywhere least subject to deterioration, whose value depended upon itself and not upon Congress, nor upon legal-tender acts, but upon free and not compulsory acceptance; that is, under the circumstances of the present time, they would choose gold and not silver.

One infallible test and measure of the soundness of metallic or other currency is to be found in the answer to the question, whether deprived of the legal-tender power guaranted it by the State it would still be sought after and voluntarily received in payment at its full nominal value. If it would, then it is plain that it is received because of some quality inherent in itself, something which the law does not endow it with and can not take from it. If it would not, then it is just as plain that it is accepted under compulsion, and that but for the coercive power of the State forcing the creditor to receive it, it would not circulate at its full nominal value. Tested in this way, it would not be long before even the owners of silver would cease advocating its use as money equally with gold and bringing it to the mints to be coined into a currency which no one was willing to receive and which would therefore remain on their hands as useless, except for employment in the arts, as if it had never been extracted from the mines. In short, in obedience to the natural law of the survival of the fittest, in the struggle of the standards for existence, the gold standard would prevail and the better money drive out the worse; for Gresham's law does not operate where the State does not make the worse money legal tender, and compel the creditor to receive it even when his self-interest would induce him to choose the better."

PREFACE. 13

As stamped since 1873, the United States silver dollar is, in fact, a token coin, just as much as a ten-cent piece or a five-cent nickel piece. A token coin is one whose metallic value is inferior to its value in the form of coin; and which, on that account, is made legal tender only to a limited amount. Its essential characteristic, however, is that it is overvalued in the coinage; and the silver dollars being thus overvalued are essentially token not standard coins; for a standard coin is one of which the value in exchange depends solely upon the value of the material contained in it. "We may," says Jevons, "treat such coins as bullion and melt them up or export them to countries where they are not legally current; yet the value of the metal, being independent of legislation, will everywhere be recognized." The metallic value of our 5-cent nickel pieces is 3.6 mills, of our 1-cent bronze pieces 1.4 mills. Both our nickel and our bronze coins are legal tender to the amount of 25 cents. At the average price of silver in 1895 the metallic value of our 50-cent piece was 23.656 cents, and of our quarters and dimes 11.828 cents and 4.73 cents respectively. The metallic value of the miscalled standard silver dollar, at the average price of silver in 1895, was 50.587 cents. Being nearly 50 per cent. below its nominal value, it was just as much a token coin as our bronze nickel, and fractional silver coins; yet the fractional silver coins are legal tender to the amount of only ten dollars, while the silver dollars must be received by the creditor in discharge of any debt, no matter how large, be it $11 or $20,000.00. It is plain to any unprejudiced mind that the false principle of finance or money which decrees that silver coins worth only 50½ cents shall be received by creditors at the rate of 100 cents, might just as well decree that nickel coins should be unlimited legal tender at the rate of 20 nickel pieces, intrinsically worth 7.2 cents, to the dollar. And it would be just as logical to agitate in favor of the free coinage of nickel as it is to defend the free coinage of silver 50-cent dollars, with the payment power of whole dollars. Who would be benefited by such a free coinage of nickel? The owners of the metal and dishonest debtors determined to discharge in dross debts contracted in gold—to bankrupt their creditors by the payment of 7.2 cents on the dollar.

No evil results attend the circulation of our nickel and bronze token coins nor of our fractional silver coins, because they are only limited legal tender. Our whole dollars, being, in fact, token coins, should, as becomes their character, be of limited legal tender to prevent their working mischief.

Unlike other token coins, however, they are, under our present monetary arrangements, full legal tender, and must be exchanged in the form of silver certificates for coins of a higher order, viz., for gold dollars, by the United States Treasury; and it is mainly to exchange the silver dollar token coins or their representatives for gold that we have borrowed in about two years $250,000,000—$125,000,000 per year—an annual expenditure likely to continue to the ruin of our commerce and the impoverishment of our people —for the interest and principal of these loans must be met by the taxation of our people. So long as we had only the legal tender notes to redeem, our gold reserve gave us no trouble. It not only did not decline to $60,000,000, or under, but was as high, at the close of the fiscal year 1887, as $186,754,217; of 1888, as $193,610,172; of 1889, as $186,711,560; and of 1890, as $190,232,404. These were the four years preceding the passage of the act of July 14, 1890. Contrast them with the amount of the reserve for the four years following, beginning with 1891, when it was at the end of the fiscal years respectively, $117,667,723, $114,342,366, $95,485,414, and $64,873,025.

It may be safely predicted that to keep our full legal tender token coins at par with gold under our present arrangements, will cost us 100 to 125 millions a year in gold, equivalent to 200–250 million dollars' worth of silver—which is only another way of saying that the more silver we put in circulation the poorer the government will become, and the more inextricably involved in debt.

We have already spent on our worthless monetary system, simply in order to keep it from becoming more worthless, an amount of money which would have supplied us with a navy infinitely superior to England's, and erected coast defences from Maine to Florida and from Alaska to California.

The great task that will confront the next national administration, be it Democratic or Republican, will be the reform of our monetary system; for that is a question that will not down. The battle of the standards is like the struggle between slavery and freedom, an irrepressible one; and like the latter it will never close until it is settled right, that is, in accordance with the principles of morality, of jurisprudence, of political economy, of commercial honor, of finance and of true American statemanship. The right settlement of the slavery question placed the Republican party in power for nearly a generation. The political supremacy of the future will belong to the party that solves the problem of monetary reform in accordance with just and scientific principles.

In conclusion, it is proper to state that Mr. Preston is in no manner responsible for any views expressed in this preface. Nor is he for the appearance of his essay on our currency legislation in its present form. The compiler did not ask Mr. Preston's consent to republish it, because had his request that he might do so been refused, he felt that the cause of a sound currency for the United States would have been the loser.

PUBLIUS.

CONTENTS.

THE MONETARY LEGISLATION AND CURRENCY SYSTEM OF THE UNITED STATES. FROM THE COLONIAL PERIOD TO 1792 . . 19
COINAGE SCHEME PROPOSED BY ROBERT MORRIS, SUPERINTENDENT OF FINANCE 21
MR. JEFFERSON'S NOTES ON THE ESTABLISHMENT OF A MONEY UNIT AND OF A COINAGE FOR THE UNITED STATES 29
REPORT OF A GRAND COMMITTEE ON THE MONEY MINT, 1785 . . 38
PROPOSITIONS RESPECTING THE COINAGE OF GOLD, SILVER AND COPPER 38
REPORT OF THE BOARD OF TREASURY, 1786 41
THE SILVER PERIOD, 1792–1834—ACT OF APRIL 2, 1792 42
REPORT OF ALEXANDER HAMILTON ON THE ESTABLISHMENT OF A MINT 42
  1. THE MONEY MINT 44
  2. THE UNIT SHOULD BE ATTACHED TO BOTH GOLD AND SILVER. 46
  3. THE COINAGE RATES OF THE TWO METALS SHOULD BE THEIR MARKET OR COMMERCIAL RATIO 48
  4. THE PROPORTION AND COMPOSITION OF ALLOY IN THE COINS. 51
  5. WHO SHOULD BEAR THE EXPENSE OF COINAGE 53
  6. FOREIGN COINS SHOULD BE TREATED AS MERCHANDISE . . . 55
  7. NUMBER, DENOMINATIONS, ETC., OF THE COINS 63
ANALYSIS OF HAMILTON'S REPORT 69
THE GOLD PERIOD, 1834–1853—ACTS OF JUNE 28, 1834, AND JANUARY 18, 1837 86

CONTENTS.

GOLD PERIOD, 1853–1873—DEMONETIZATION OF SILVER BY THE
ACT OF FEBRUARY 21, 1853 89
THE LEGAL TENDER NOTES 93
THE NATIONAL BANK NOTES 96
GOLD PERIOD, 1873–1878—DEMONETIZATION OF SILVER IN 1873. 96
HON. JOHN SHERMAN ADVOCATES THE SINGLE GOLD STANDARD,
WITH SILVER AS LIMITED LEGAL TENDER 97
THE PERIOD OF THE LIMPING STANDARD, 1878, TO THE PRESENT
TIME, ACTS OF 1878 AND 1890 101
REFORM OF OUR CURRENCY SYSTEM 105
THE FREE COINAGE OF SILVER 114
HON. JAMES H. ECKELS' SPEECH 119

THE MONETARY LEGISLATION

AND

CURRENCY SYSTEM OF THE UNITED STATES.

FROM THE COLONIAL PERIOD TO 1792.

ANTERIOR to the adoption of the Constitution, the thirteen American Colonies had, like England, the silver standard, and their metallic circulating medium consisted of foreign coins. The unit of account was the Spanish "milled dollar" or piece of eight (pieza de ocho.) Up to about 1775, however, accounts were kept in pounds, shillings, and pence—a pound consisting then, as now, of 20 shillings, and a shilling of 12 pence "Colonial" or "pound currency," $133\frac{1}{3}$ pounds of which were equal to 100 pounds sterling. Four pounds "Colonial currency" were, therefore, equal to 3 pounds sterling. This par of the Colonial and the sterling pound was established by the fact that the Spanish piaster, or milled dollar, was worth, in the Colonies, 6 shillings, while in England it was valued at only $4\frac{1}{2}$ shillings. Calculated in accordance with the legal weight and fineness of the Spanish silver piaster (up to 1772, $8\frac{1}{2}$ pieces from the gross Castilian marco 0.909722 fine), the "pound currency" was a quantity of 82.069960 grams, or 1,296.508715 grains of fine silver.

Besides the Spanish milled dollar there was a variety of other foreign coins in circulation, but in keeping accounts the pound and the shilling came next in order of common usage to the dollar. The method by which the Colonial composite system of current coins was regulated consisted in coinage tariffs, so much in vogue in early European monetary history. Such a tariff, issued in 1750, valued the ounce of silver at 6 shillings 8 pence and the Spanish milled dollar at 6 shillings, the guinea at 28 shillings, and the English crown at 6 shillings 8 pence. In this tariff all foreign coins were valued in proportion to the Spanish piece of eight, it being considered that many and great inconveniences would arise in case any coined silver or gold, or English half-pence and farthings, should pass current at any higher rate than in just proportion to that piece. The shilling was stamped by some of the colonies and constituted a large part of the money in circulation. It, however, varied greatly in value in the different Colonies. Thus, the Spanish dollar equalled 5 shillings in Georgia; 8 shillings in North Carolina and New York (12½ cents); 6 shillings in Virginia, Connecticut, New Hampshire, Massachusetts, and Rhode Island (16⅔ cents); 7 shillings 6 pence in Maryland, Delaware, Pennsylvania, and New Jersey; 32 shillings 6 pence in South Carolina. This accounts for the present reckoning of 12½ cents to a "shilling" in New York, Ohio, etc., and of 16⅔ cents in New England and Virginia.

The following coinage tariff was published in 1776 in the report of a special committee, appointed in April of that year:

Description.	Weight.		Value.
	Dwt.	*Grs.*	
English guinea	5	6	$4.66⅔
French guinea	5	5	4.62½
Johannes	18	0	16.00
Half-johannes	9	0	8.00
Spanish pistole	4	8	3.66⅔
French pistole	4	4	3.50
Moidore	6	18	6.00
English crown			1.11½
French crown			1.11½
English shilling			.22¼

This same tariff rated gold bullion at $17 per ounce, troy weight, and sterling silver at $1.11⅛ per ounce.

The Spanish dollar, with which this comparison was made, was itself not unfrequently below the legal weight, and therefore varied in value.

If the pieces mentioned in the coinage tariff of 1776 were of full weight, the ratio there established was the English ratio of 1 to 15.21. The ratio for bullion was not materially different.

The tariff of 1776 had been in operation six years when the Colonies began to feel keenly the diffiulties caused by the variety of coins constituting their metallic circulating medium, as well as its injurious effects on business and on the methods of keeping accouuts.

The need of a special American coinage was frequently expressed, and in 1782 (15th of January) Robert Morris, the Superintendent of Finance, at the request of a committee of the Congress of the Confederation, submitted a scheme for a national coinage and for the establishment of an American mint, which met with its approval. Morris's report is here given in full:

COINAGE SCHEME PROPOSED BY ROBERT MORRIS, SUPERINTENDENT OF FINANCE.

[From MS. letters and reports of the Superintendent of Finance, No. 137, volume 1, pages 289-300.]

OFFICE OF FINANCE, *January 15, 1782.*

SIR: Finding by the act of the United States in Congress, of the seventh instant, that I am instructed to prepare and report a table of rates at which the different species of foreign coins most likely to circulate in the United States shall be received at the Treasury, I have been induced again to turn my attention to an object which has employed my thoughts very frequently, and which would have long since been submitted to Congress, had I not been prevented by other business, and much delayed by the things, relating to this business, which depended upon others. I shall now pray leave to deliver my sentiments somewhat at large on this subject.

The United States labor under many inconveniences, and even disadvantages, which may at present be remedied; but which, if suffered to continue, would become incurable, and lead to pernicious consequences. It is very fortunate for us, that the weights aud measures used throughout America are the same; experience has shown in other Countries, that the efforts of the Legislator to change Weights and

Measures, altho' fully seconded by the more enlightened part of the community, have been so strongly opposed by the popular habits and prejudices, that ages have elapsed without producing the desired effect. I repeat therefore that, it is happy for us to have throughout the Union, the same ideas of a mile and an inch, a Hogshead and a quart, a pound and an ounce. So far our commercial dealings are simplified, and brought down to the level of every capacity.

With respect to our money the case is very widely different. The ideas annexed to a pound, shilling, and a penny, are almost as various as the States themselves. Calculations are therefore as necessary for our inland commerce as upon foreign exchanges; and the commonest things become intricate where money has anything to do with them. A Farmer in New Hampshire, for instance, can readily form an idea of a bushel of wheat in South Carolina, weighing sixty pounds, and placed at one hundred miles from Charleston; but if he were told that in such situation it is worth twenty-one shillings and eight pence, he would be obliged to make many inquiries, and form some calculations before he would know that this sum meant, in general, what he would call four shillings; and even then he would to enquire what kind of coin that four shillings was paid in, before he could estimate it in his own mind according to the ideas of money which he had imbibed.

Difficulties of this sort do not occur to farmers alone, they are perplexing to most men, and troublesome to all; it is, however, a fortunate circumstance, that money is so much in the power of the Sovereign, that he can easily lead the people into new ideas of it; and even if that were not the case, yet the loose state in which our currency has been for some years past, has opened the way for receiving any impressions on that subject. As we are now shaking off the inconveniences of a depreciating medium, the present moment seems to be that in which a general currency can best be established, so as that in a few months, the same names of money will mean the same things, in the several parts of the United States.

Another inconvenience, which admits of the same easy remedy, and which could, indeed, be cured by the very same act, is the want of a legal tender. This is as necessary for the purposes of jurisprudence, as a general currency is for those of commerce. For although there is a great impropriety, not to say injustice, in compelling a man to receive a part of his debt in discharge of the whole; yet it is both just and proper that the law should protect the honest debtor who is willing to pay, against the vexatious suits of an oppressive creditor, who refuses to receive the full value.

The nature, value and use of money have always occasioned strong temptations to the commission of Fraud; and of consequence the practice of counterfeiting is coeval with that of coining.

No Government can guard its subjects entirely against the wicked Ingenuity which has been exercised in this respect; But it has always been the object of every wise government to take all the precautions against it which are within the compass of human ability. These precautions will be most effectual where the coins are few and simple; because they, by that means, become familiar to all ranks and degrees of men; but where the coins are so numerous that the knowledge of them is a kind of science, the lower order of citizens are constantly injured by those, who carry on the business of debasing, sweating, counterfeiting and the like. It is therefore to be lamented that we have so many different coins in the United States.

It is not necessary to mention what is in every bodies mouth, that the precious metals were first used as Bullion, and that the inconvenience of weighing and the difficulty of assaying, introducing the practtce of coining, in order that the weight and fineness might be known at the first view, and of consequence the value be instantly ascertained. It is equally unnecessary to observe, that the great privilege of declaring this value, by particular marks, has among all nations been vested, exclusively in the sovereign. A trust so important could not indeed be vested any where else, because the danger of abusing it was too great; and history informs us, that Sovereigns themselves have not on this occasion behaved with that integrity, which was alike due to their subjects and to themselves, to the interests of the people, and to their own personal glory.

Experience has already told us, that the advantage of Gold as a coin, is in this country very considerably diminished; for every distinct piece must be weighed before it can be safely received.

Both Gold and silver coins are indeed preferable in one respect to common Bullion, that the standard is presumed to be just, and consequently they are received without the delays and expenses of assaying. It must however be remembered, that they are foreign Coins, and of course we are not only exposed to the tricks of individuals, but should it suit the interest or convenience of any sovereign to make base money for us, there is nothing to prevent it. If for instance, the King of England, or any of his Birmingham artists, should coin Guineas worth but sixteen shillings sterling, our citizens would readily and freely receive them at twenty-one shillings sterling. It is my duty to mention to Congress information I have received, that Guineas of base metal are coined at Birmingham so well, as to escape any common attention. Now there can be no doubt that every such Guinea received here, would be a national loss to us, of an English crown. How much we suffer in this way at present, it is impossible to estimate. What I have already had the honor to observe contains some of the reasons, why it appears to me highly necessary that an American coin should be adopted without delay; and to these reasons it may be added that there is a want of small money for the common occasions of trade and that it is more felt by our Soldiery, than any other persons. For the little pay which they *do* receive, being either in gold or at best in dollars, the sutlers and others with whom they have dealings, continually take the advantage of their want of change, and rate the prices of their goods accordingly.

Shortly after my appointment, finding that there was a considerable quantity of public Copper at Boston, I ordered it round to this place. It has safely arrived, and will when coined amount to a considerable sum. The necessary machinery of a mint can be easily made, and there are persons who can perform the whole business. I must pray leave, therefore, to submit to Congress, some few more particular remarks on this subject, an introductory to a plan for an American coin.

Although most nations have coined Copper, yet that metal is so impure that it has never been considered as constituting the Money Standard. This is affixed to the two precious metals, because they alone will admit of having their intrinsic value precisely ascertained; but nations differ very much in the relation they have established between Gold and Silver. In some European countries an ounce of pure Gold passes for fifteen ounces of pure Silver; in others for fourteen. In China it passes for much less. The standard, therefore, which is affixed to both metals is in reality affixed to neither. In England Gold is to Silver nearly in the proportion of one to fifteen, and in France nearly one to fourteen. If a man carries fourteen ounces of Gold from France to England, he receives two hundred and ten ounces of Silver, which in France purchases fifteen ounces of Gold, so that he gains on that exchange one ounce of Gold. In like manner he who carries from England fourteen ounces of Silver to France, recives one ounce of Gold, which in England purchases fifteen ounces of Silver, wherefore he gains on that exchange one ounce of Silver.

If it be then supposed that the coins of these two countries were alike pure, it must follow that in a short time all the Gold coin of full weight would be in England; and all the Silver coin of full weight in France. But the light Silver circulating in England and the light Gold in France, the real standard of coin in each would be different from the legal, and seek a medium of fourteen and a half of Silver for one of Gold, altho' the legal standard might still be in the one place fifteen, and in the other fourteen.

The demand which commerce might make for any one of the precious metals in preference of the other, would vary this real standard from time to time, and in every payment a man would get more or less of real value for his debt, according as he was paid in coin of greater or lesser value, in relation to the real standard. If, for instance, the debt were contracted when the Silver was to Gold, as one to fifteen, and paid when as one to fourteen; If the debt were paid in Silver he would gain one thirtieth, and if in Gold he would lose one thirtieth. In England the money standard is rather affixed to Gold than to Silver, because all payments are made in the former, and in France it is rather affixed to Silver than to Gold.

Arguments are unnecessary to show that the scale by which everything is to be measured ought to be as fixed as the nature of things will permit of. Since therefore, a money standard affixed to both the precious metals will not give the certain scale, it is better to make use of one only. Gold is more valuable than Silver, and so far must have the preference, but it is from that very circumstance the more exposed to fradulent practices. Its value rendering it more portable is an advantage, but it is an advantage which paper possesses in a much greater degree, and of consequence the commercial nation of England has had recourse to paper for the purpose of its Trade; although the mass of circulating Coin is Gold. It will always be in our power to carry a paper circulation to every proper extent. There can be no doubt therefore, that our money standard ought to be affixed to Silver. But Silver is liable like everything else, to a change of value; if there is a demand for it, to export, the value will raise, if the contrary it will fall, and so far it cannot be considered as a fixed measure of value. Before this objection be considered it will be proper to make a few reflections on another part of the present subject, but in this place I remark, that if the objection cannot be removed we must not suffer it to preponderate, because it weighs alike against every other metal.

To coin money is a certain expense, and of course it is an expense which must be borne by the people. In England the coin when melted, will sell as Bullion for just as much as its weight in other coin. The expense of coinage is paid by the Crown, and of course it is raised by taxes from the people. In France the Coinage instead of being expensive, yields a profit.

The price given for metal at the mint is about eight per cent. less than the same quantity will yield when coined at the French Standard; both of these methods are liable to objections. When commerce demands àn exportation of Bullion from England, the Coin of the kingdom goes out in common with others; this increases, of course, the national expense of coinage. Laws to prevent the exportation or importation of anything so valuable as money, are always nugatory, because they always *can* be eluded, and, therefore, when private interests requires, they always *will* be eluded. That the Guineas of England, therefore, are not continnally going away, is to be attributed to the extraordinary value affixed to Gold, which has just been mentioned, and which banishes Silver continually.

In France the people are not liable to this inconvenience, because their Money passing for more than its value in Bullion, Bullion will always be exported in preference of coin; but for the same reason, there is always a strong temptation to imitate their coin, and send it for the purchase of their commodities. It would be both impossible and unnecessary to distinguish the true from the false, because both would be of equal intrinsic value; the place at which they were struck would be indifferent to the receiver, of consequence the foreigner who made French coin would gain by his trade, and the French nation would lose proportionately.

The money paid for coining, or the coinage of France, has, however, this advantage, that the Money is a standard which does not fluctuate with the price of Bultion. This coining is, as has been said, about 8 per cent. When Bullion is below ninety-two it is carried to the Mint, when above ninety-two to the Broker or Silversmith. The Coin still continues fixed, nor will it bear exportation until Bullion rises to an hundred, when the French Coin would be as liable to exportation as the English. In that case it would be exported on one hand, while on the other no more would have been coined for a considerable period, because to make the 8 per cent. coinage it is necessary that the Mint price should be ninety-two. The Coin therefore could not long be exported, if at all, but would soon resume its value. The price of Bullion must float between ninety-two and an hundred, while the Coin would preserve its fixed quality as Money.

Hence, then, it appears proper that the price of coining should be defrayed by the coinage, because, first, it is natural and proper, that the price should be paid when the benefit is received, and that the citizen in return for the advantage of being ascertained in the value of the medium of commerce by the sovereign should pay for ascertaining it just as he should pay for the fashion of the plate he uses, or the construction of the cart he employs.

Secondly, It is right that money should acquire a value as money, distinct from that which it possesses as a commodity, in order that it should be a fixed rule whereby to measure the value of all other things; and, thirdly, it is wise to prevent the exportation of the coin, which would involve an unnecessary national expense, and also to prevent the imitation of it abroad, so as to create a national loss; for both which purposes it is proper that the coinage should only defray the expense, without making any considerable profit. The Laws usual in all countries with respect to the money will then fully operate the effect intended.

In order that a coin may be perfectly intelligible to the whole people, it must have some affinity to the former currency.

This, therefore, will be requisite in the present case. The purposes of commerce require that the lowest divisible point of money or what is more properly called the money unit should be very small; because by that means price can be brought in the smallest things to bear a proportion to the value, and altho' it is not absolutely necessary, yet it is very desirable that money should be increased in a decimal Ratio, because by that means all calculations of Interest, exchange, insurance and the like are rendered much more simple and accurate, and, of course, more within the power of the great mass of people. Whenever such things require much labor, time and reflection, the greater number who do not know, are made the dupes of the lesser number who do.

The various coins which have circulated in America have undergone different changes in their value, so that there is hardly any which can be considered as a general Standard, unless it be Spanish dollars; these pass in Georgia at five shillings, in North Carolina and New York at eight shillings, in Virginia and the four Eastern States at six shillings, in all the other States except South Carolina at seven shillings and sixpence, and in South Carolina at thirty-two shillings and sixpence. The money unit of a new coin to agree without a fraction with all these different values of a dollar except the last, will be the fourteen hundred and fortieth part of a dollar, equal to the sixteenth hundredth part of a crown; of these units twenty-four will be a penny of Georgia; fifteen will be a penny of North Carolina or New York; twenty will be a penny of Virginia and the four Eastern States; sixteen will be a penny of all the other States except South Carolina, and forty-eight will be thirteen pence of South Carolina. It has been already observed, that to have the money unit very small is advantageous to commerce; but there is no necessity that this money unit be exactly represented in coin; it is sufficient that its value be precisely known. On the present occasion, two copper coins will be proper; the one of eight units, and the other of five. These may be called an eight and a five; two of the former will make a penny proclamation or Pennsylvania money; and three a penny Georgia money; of the latter three will make a penny York money; and four a penny lawful or Virginia money. The money unit will be equal to a quarter of a grain of fine Silver in coined money: Proceeding thence in a decimal ratio, one hundred would be the lowest Silver coin and might be called a cent. It would contain twenty-five grains of fine Silver, to which may be added two grains of copper, and the whole would weigh one pennyweight three grains: Five of these would make a quint or five hundred units, weighing five pennyweight fifteen grains; and ten would make a mark or one thousand units weighing eleven pennyweight six grains.

If the mint price of fine Silver be established at 22.237 units per pound; this, being coined, would be four times 5.760 grains or 23.040 units; the difference is 803 units, and, therefore, the coinage is 803 on 23.040, or somewhat more, than 3.48 per cent., which would be about the expense attending it. A Dollar contains by the best assays which I have been able to get, about 373 grains of fine Silver, and that at the mint price would be 1,440 units. In like manner, if Crowns contain from 414 to 415 grains of fine Silver, they would at the mint price be worth 1,600 units.

When such a Coin shall have been established, the value of all others would be easily ascertained, because nothing more would be necessary than to have them assayed at the mint. The advantage of possessing legal money in preference of any other, would induce people to carry foreign Coin to the mint, until a sufficiency were struck for the circulating medium. The remainder of the foreign Silver, together with the Gold, should be left, entirely to the operations of Commerce as Bullion.

In the present moment it is by no means of such consequence to establish the relative value of different Coins, as to provide a standard of our own by which in future to estimate them. If the value were now sought they must all be estimated in dollars, because dollars are called for in the several requisitions of Congress. Without noticing the preference, thus given to one foreign Coin over another, it is sufficient to observe, that if a greater alloy should be introduced by the Spanish Government into their dollars our interior Regulations as to money would be overturned, and certainly we have no security that this will not happen. There is not any great inconvenience from leaving matters on their present footing until they can be remedied by the operations of a mint; for it is not to be supposed that all the money raised by Taxes in a State is to be brought out of it. I expect that there will be very little occasion to transport money from place to place. It is much easier to negotiate than to carry it; and if any species of Money is generally received within a State at the same rate in which it is paid in Taxes, there will be no difficulty in expending it at its value. Whenever Money shall be struck by Authority of the United States, then indeed it will be proper to receive in Taxes no other Coin.

If Congress are of opinion with me, that it will be proper to coin Money, I will immediately obey their orders and establish a mint; and I think I can say with safety that no better moment could be chosen for the purpose than the present; neither will anything have a greater tendency to restore public credits, for although it is possible that the new money will at first be received with diffidence by some, yet when it has been fairly assayed it will gain full confidence from all, and the advantage of holding the only Money which can pay debts or discharge Taxes, will soon give it the preference over all, and indeed banish all other from Circulation; whereas, fixing a Relation of value now, on whatever principles attempted, might give offense to the Power whose Coin should in any instance be reduced from its present numerary value among us. These sentiments are submitted with all possible deference to the United States in Congress Assembled in expectation of their further instructions on the subject.

With great Respect I have the honor to be, sir your most obedient and humble servant,[1]

ROB. MORRIS.

---

[1] The financial condition of the United States in its early days scarcely comes within the scope of an article on the monetary legislation and currency system of

Jefferson, like Morris, recommended the decimal system, but advocated the dollar as the unit. It is probable that Mr. Jefferson's Notes on the Establishment of a Money Unit and of a Coinage for the United States were communicated to Congress at the same time as Mr. Morris's letter reproduced above. The document containing them is not

the United States, and yet is a subject so closely related to it and to the life and labors of Robert Morris, Superintendent of Finance, that an account of our general financial situation at that period is but a complement to the history of our monetary legislation at the same time. The following extract from the eulogy by the Hon. John G. Carlisle, Secretary of the Treasury, delivered on the occasion of the dedication of the Old Holland Land Office Building, in Batavia, N. Y., October 13, 1894, finds a very appropriate place here:

"At that time there was no Treasury Department, nor any national executive organization of any kind. Early in 1779 the Continental Congress had appointed a standing committee, of which James Duane was chairman, to superintend the finances, but its functions were not well defined, and its duties, so far as it had any, were loosely and negligently discharged. By September, 1778, financial affairs had fallen into such a condition of confusion and disorder that Congress established five separate bureaus to assist in the management of the Treasury; but these bureaus quarreled with each other, and in 1779 an ordinance was passed establishing what was designated as a Board of Treasury, consisting of three commissioners, not Members of Congress, and two members of Congress, any two of whom had power to transact business. By the spring of 1780, however, it became evident that the entire financial system must be reorganized upon a more substantial basis, and that there must be such practical management as would secure order in the public accounts and some degree of economy in the public service, or the war would prove a disastrous failure and the Colonies relapse into a more hopeless condition of dependency than ever existed before.

"Almost every financial expedient that the ingenuity of man could devise, except regular and effective taxation, had been resorted to for nearly six years to raise money or procure credit for the prosecution of war, and at last the very verge of national bankruptcy had been reached and it was evidently impossible to proceed a step farther in the same direction without a total collapse of the entire financial system, involving, of course, an abandonment of the struggle. The country was smothered to death under a mass of worthless paper currency far more disastrous to the commercial and industrial interests of the people than all the spoilations and devastations committed by the invading enemy. The most discreditable chapters of our history are those which record the repeated and ineffectual efforts of the Continental Congress and the Superintendent of Finance, after he was chosen, to induce the States to raise their respective quotas of money necessary to carry on a war for the establishment of their own independence. The prevailing idea among the people seemed to be that, inasmuch as the war dated, but it was presumably written in 1782 or 1783, and is as follows:

MR. JEFFERSON'S NOTES ON THE ESTABLISHMENT OF A MONEY UNIT AND OF A COINAGE FOR THE UNITED STATES.

[In fixing the unit of money these circumstances are of a principal importance.]
1. That it be of a convenient size to be applied as a measure to the common money transactions of life.

---

was being prosecuted in opposition to the claim of Great Britain to impose taxes upon them, it would be illogical and inconsistent to impose taxes upon themselves. They prefered to rely upon Continential notes, issued in anticipation of receipts which never came in, and upon bills of credit emitted by the States, which persistently refused to provide funds for their redemption. The several Colonies had been in the habit, long before the Revolution, of issuing their own notes to circulate as money, and therefore the Continental Congress very naturally resorted to the same expedient, and the first notes, amounting to about $3,000,000, were issued as early as 1775. These notes began to depreciate almost immediately, and before the close of the year 1776 many men were subject to mob violence, to social and political ostracism, and to imprisonment by the civil and military authorities for refusing to receive them in payment of debt or in exchange for commodities.

"By 1779 depreciation had gone to such an extent that it was no longer safe to buy and sell in the ordinary way, while transactions conducted upon credit were ruinous to the party who rendered services or parted with his property. Barter was the only safe trade, and it is recorded that at one time it was substantially the only kind of trade carried on in the city of Boston. Prices went up so that a pair of shoes cost $100, and flour sold at prices ranging from $400 to $500 per hundredweight. The price of sugar reached $600 per hundredweight, coffee was $4 per pound, and wheat $75 per bushel, and the cost of most articles of necessity rose in the same proportion. General Washington said that a wagon load of money would scarcely buy a wagon load of provisions. But the currency in which payments were made was depreciating with such rapidity that the merchant who sold even at these extraordinary prices was constantly losing money. The injurious effect of a depreciating currency upon the trade of the country is illustrated in the case of a writer of that period, who says that he purchased a hogshead of sugar and sold it at a large profit, but the currency in which he was paid would buy only a tierce. He then sold the tierce at a large profit, but when he used the proceeds of his sale in making another purchase he got only a barrel. R. H. Lee wrote to Thomas Jefferson that the depreciation of money had nearly transferred his whole estate to his tenants, and that the rent of 4,000 acres of land would not pay for 20 bushels of corn, the rent, of course, being payable in money and having been fixed before the depreciation began.

"Conventions were held in many parts of the country to establish scales of prices at which commodities should be bought and sold, and several States enacted penal laws upon the subject. Many merchants and others were punished

2. That its parts and multiples be in an easy proportion to each other so as to facilitate the Money Arithmetic.

3. That the Unit and its parts or divisions be so nearly of the value of some of the known coins as that they may be of easy adoption for the people.

The Spanish Dollar seems to fulfill all these conditions.

1. Taking into our view all money transactions great and small, I question if a common measure of more convenient size than the dollar can be proposed. The value of 100, 1,000, 10,000 dollars is well estimated by the mind; so is that of the 10th or the hundredth of a dollar. Few transactions are above or below these limits. The expediency of attending to the size of the money Unit will be evident to any one who will consider how inconvenient it would be to a manufacturer or merchant, if, instead of the yard for measuring cloth, either the inch or the mill had been made the unit of measure.

---

by imprisonment and by exposure in the pillory for violations of these statutes, and necessarily much ill-feeling was engendered among the people. The whole commercial fabric was in imminent danger of destruction on account of the superabundance of so-called money, and the Government itself, which possessed unlimited power to issue it, was compelled to retrace its steps, or be crushed under the weight of its own paper. * * *

"At this time Continental notes had been issued to the amount of $160,000,000, or about $53 per capita, and the depreciation was 30 to 1; that is, $1 in specie was equal to $30 in paper currency. By July, 1780, it was 64.12 to 1, and early in the next year the whole miserable system broke completely down, and Congress, with only one dissenting voice, resolved that all debts then due from the United States which had been liquidated according to their value, and all debts which had been, or should thereafter be, made payable in specie should be actually paid in specie or its equivalent at the current rate of exchange between specie and other currency. The total issue of Continental notes up to that date, as nearly as can be ascertained, was about $242,000,000, or $80 per capita.

But, besides this, the various States had issued large amounts in bills of credit, and there were outstanding large amounts of loan-office certificates and quartermasters' and commissaries' certificates, which greatly aggravated the financial situation. It is said that in 1788 a single Spanish dollar would legally discharge a debt of $2,400 in the State of Virginia. The resolution of Congress was absolutely necessary in order to save even a semblance of public credit, and although the Contiuental notes continued for a short time to circulate in some parts of the country, especially in the South, they passed for merely a fraction of their nominal value. It was evident to every one at all acquainted with public affairs that the finances of the country must at once be placed in more competent hands and conducted with more vigor and economy than had heretofore characterized their management or that the war for independence would be brought to a speedy termination by the complete subjugation of the Colonies. The opinion was quite prevalent, both in America and Europe, that the struggle could be maintained but a little while longer, and even General Washington had almost abandoned all hope of success.

2. The most easy ratio of multiplication and division is that by ten. Every one knows the facility of decimal arithmetic. Every one remembers that when learning money arithmetic, he used to be puzzled with adding the farthings, taking out the fours and carrying them on, adding the pence, taking out the twelves and carrying them on; adding the shillings, taking out the twenties and carrying them on; but when he came to the pounds, when he had only tens to carry forward, it was easy and free from error.

The bulk of mankind are school-boys thro' life. These little perplexities are always great to them. And even mathematical heads feel the relief of an easier substituted for a more difficult process. Foreigners, too, who have trade or who travel among us will find a great facility in understanding our coins and accounts from this ratio of subdivision, Those who have had occasion to convert the livres,

---

"George III and his ministers relied for success more upon the depressed financial condition of the United States than upon the aggressive operations of their army and navy. This was the condition of affairs when Congress, on the 20th of February, 1781, unanimously chose Robert Morris to be Superintendent of Finance. His great ability and credit as a merchant, his intimate acquaintance with public matters generally, and especially his familiarity with the financial operations which had reduced the Government to such a deplorable state of poverty and helplessness, constituted qualifications for this laborious and responsible position possessed by no other man in the country. The selection at once revived the hopes of the despondent, stimulated the courage of the wavering, and confirmed the faith of the friends of liberty in every part of the world. But he did not accept at once. He knew the magnitude of the task he was expected to perfnrm, and he knew it could not be accomplished unless he was afforded opportunities and invested with powers commensurate with the nature of the duties imposed upon him. He therefore wrote a letter to the President of Congress in which he made the acceptance of the office dependent upon two conditions: First, that he should not be required to abandon his commercial pursuits or dissolve his existing connections with certain mercantile establishments; and secondly, that he should have the absolute power to appoint and remove all officials serving under him. Upon this point he was very emphatic.

* * * * * * * * *

"Congress having, after some hesitation, conformed to the wishes of Morris in respect to these two matters, he accepted the office on the 14th day of May, 1781, but did not enter fully upon the discharge of his duties until October following. In June, 1781, before he had taken charge of his office, he secured the repeal of the embargo law, believing, to use his own language, that 'commerce should be perfectly free and property sacredly secure to the owner.' He applied himself with zeal and determination to the difficult task imposed upon him, and the result of his labors soon began to be felt in all the affairs of the Government at home and abroad, and in all the business transactions of the people. The extent and variety of the powers vested in him and the number and character of the various kinds of business transacted by him on the public account have no parallel in the history of any other financial officer in the world. He was, in fact, the

sols and deniers of the French, the Gilders Stivers and penings of the Dutch, the pounds, shillings, pence and farthings of these several states into each other can judge how much they would have aided had their several subdivisions been in a decimal ratio. Certainly in all cases where we are free to chuse between easy and difficult modes of operation, it is most rational to chuse the easy. The financier therefore in his report well proposes that our coins should be in decimal proportions to one another. If we adopt the dollar for our unit, we should strike four coins, one of gold, two of silver, and one of copper, viz:

1. A Golden piece equal in value to 10 dollars.
2. The unit or dollar itself, of silver.
3. The tenth of a dollar, of silver also.
4. The hundredth of a dollar of copper.

Compare the arithmetical operations on the same sum of money expressed in this form, & expressed in the pound sterling and its divisions:

---

autocrat of finances. He engaged in a great number of mercantile enterprises on account of the Government, buying and selling goods here and in other countries, and using the proceeds in the public service. Congress had declared that the obligations of the Government should be paid in specie, or its equivalent, but the Government had no specie and no visable means of procuring it. It is true that considerable specie, or hard money, as it was then called, had been brought into the country and disbursed by the British and French armies, but it had not reached the Treasury. The worthless paper currency was now rapidly disappearing from circulation, and Morris took measures to obtain a supply of specie from Havana and other places, which he accomplished to a very considerable extent by buying and selling goods. In a short time the people began to realize the benefits of that inflexible law of trade and finance under which sound money in sufficient quantities to transact all the business of the country will always make its appearance to take the place of unsound money if the latter can be got out of circulation.

"It was not long until specie was circulating in all the channels of trade, and from that time to the close of the Revolutionary war all the business of the Government was conducted upon a specie basis. There was then no American dollar nor American coin of any denomination. The principle coin in use was the Spanish dollar, the Seville piece of eight, and the Mexican piece of eight, each of which was rated at 4 shillings 6 pence sterling, and the pillar piece, which was rated at 4 shillings 6 pence 3 farthings. But the actual unit of account in America was an imaginary dollar, supposed to contein 24¾ grains of fine gold, There was, in fact, no such coin, and never had been, but this quantity of fine gold was apparently, by common consent, recognized as the standard by which the value of the various kinds of currency in circulation was measured and by which exchange was regulated."

* * * * * * * * *

Addition.

```
 £   s.   d.  [Dollars.]
 8   13   11½ = 38.65
 4   12    8¾ = 20.61
 ----------     -----
13    6    8¼ = 59.26
```

Subtraction.

```
 £   s.   d.  [Dollars.]
 8   13   11½ = 38.65
 4   12    8¾ = 20.61
 ----------     -----
 4    1    2¾ = 18.04
```

Multiplication by 8.

```
      [£    s.   d. qrs. Dollars.]
       8    13   11½ = 38.65
      20                    8
     ----               -----
     173                309.2 D
      12
     ----
    2087 or     8   13.11½
       4                 8
     ----      -----------
    8350        69   11   8
       8
    -----
   66800
    -----
¼  16700
    -----
1/12  1391 8
    -----
1/20 [£]69 11 8
```

Division by 8.

```
   [£    s.   d. qrs. Dollars.]
    8    13   11½ = 38.65
   20              8)-----
  ----                4.83
  173
   12
  ----
 2087
    4
  ----
8)8350
  ----
4)1043 6/8
  ----
12)260¾
   --
 20)21.8
   --
[£] 1.1.8¾
```

A bare inspection of the above operation will evince the labour which is occasioned by subdividing the unit into 20ths 240ths and 960ths as the English do and as we have done; and the case of subdivisions in a decimal ratio. The same difference arises in making payment. An Englishman to pay £8.13.11½ must find by calculation what combination of the coins of His country will pay this sum. But an American having the same sum to pay thus expressed 38.65 will know by inspection only that three golden pieces 8 units or dollars 6 tenths and 5 coppers pay it precisely.

3. The third condition required is that the unit, its multiples and subdivisions coincide in value with some of the known coin so nearly, that the people may by a quick reference in the mind estimate their value. If this be not attended to, they will be very long in adopting the innovation, if ever they adopt it. Let us examine in this point of view each of the four coins proposed.

1. The golden piece will be ⅙ more than a half Joe* and 1/15 more than a double guinea. It will be readily estimated then by reference to either of them but more readily and accurately as equal to 10 dollars.

2. The unit or dollar is a known coin and the most familiar of all to the mind, of the people. It is already adopted from South to North, has identified our currency and therefore happily offers itself as a Unit already introduced. Our public

* The "Half-Joe," or piece of 6400 rees was a Portuguese coin 22 carats fine weighing one half ounce of Portugal, equal to about 221 grains Troy.

debt, our requisitions and their apportionments have given it actual and long possession of the place of Unit. The course of our commerce too will bring us more of this than of any other foreign coin, and therefore renders it more worthy of attention. I know of no Unit which can be proposed in competition with the dollar, but the pound: But what is the pound? 1547 grains of fine silver in Georgia; 1289 grains in Virginia, Connecticut, Rhode Island, Massachusetts and New Hampshire; 1031¼ grains in Maryland, Delaware, Pennsylvania and New Jersey; 966¾ grains in North Carolina and New York.

Which of these shall we adopt? To which State give that pre-eminence of which all are so jealous? And on which impose the difficulties of a new estimate for their coin, their cattle and other commodities? Or shall we hang the pound sterling as a common badge about all their necks? This contains 1718¾ grains of pure silver. It is difficult to familiarize a new coin to a people. It is more difficult to familiarize them to a new coin with an old name. Happily the Dollar is familiar to them all, and is already as much referred to for a measure of value as their respective State [provincial] pounds.

3. The tenth will be precisely the Spanish bit or half pistreen in some of the States, and in others will differ from it but a very small fraction. This is a coin perfectly familiar to us all. When we shall make a new coin then equal in value to this, it will be of ready estimate with the people.

4. The hundredth or copper will be very nearly the penny or copper of New York and North Carolina, this being $\frac{1}{100}$ of a dollar, and will not be very different from the penny or copper of New Jersey, Pennsylvania, Delaware and Maryland, which is $\frac{1}{90}$ of a dollar. It will be about the medium between the old and the new coppers of these States, and therefore will soon be substituted for them both. In Virginia coppers have never been in use. It will be as easy therefore to introduce them there of one value as of another. The copper coin proposed will be nearly equal to three-fourths of their penny, which is the same with the penny lawful of the Eastern States. A great deal of small change is useful in a State, and tends to reduce the price of small articles. Perhaps it would not be amiss, to coin three [two] more pieces of silver, one of the value of five-tenths or half a dollar, one of the value of two-tenths which would be equal to the Spanish pistreen, and one of the value of 5 coppers, which would be equal to the Spanish half bit. We should then have four silver coin, viz:

1. The Unit or Dollar.
2. The half dollar or five tenths [omitted in the printed copy].
3. The double tenth, equal to 2 or ⅕ of a dollar to a pistreen.
4. The tenth, equal to a Spanish bit.
5. The five copper piece equal to 05 or $\frac{1}{20}$ of a dollar or to the half bit.

The plan reported by the financier is worthy of his sound judgment. It admits however of objection in the size of the unit. He proposes that this shall be the 1440th part of a dollar; so that it will require 1440 of his units to make them the one before proposed. He was led to adopt this by a mathematical attention to our old currencies, all of which this unit will measure without leaving a fraction. But as our object is to get rid of those currencies, the advantage derived from this coincidence will soon be past. Whereas the inconveniences of this unit will for-

MONETARY LEGISLATION.

ever remain, if they do not altogether prevent its introduction. It is defective in two of the three requisites of a money Unit.

1. It is inconvenient in its application to the ordinary money transactions. 10,000 will require 8 figures to express them, to wit, 14,400,000. A horse or bullock of 80 dollars value will require a notation of six figures, to wit 115,200 units. As a money of account this will be laborious even when facilitated by the aid of decimal arithmetic. As a common measure of the value of property it will be too minute to be comprehended by the people. The French are subjected to very laborious calculations, the livre being their ordinary money of account, and this but between the $\frac{1}{5}$ & $\frac{1}{6}$ of a dollar. But what will be our labours should our money of account be $\frac{1}{1440}$ of a dollar only?

2. It is neither equal nor near to any of the known coins in value.

If we determine that a dollar shall be our Unit, we must then say with precision what a dollar is. This coin as struck at different times, of different weights and fineness is of different values. Sir Isaac Newton's Assay and representation to the lords of the treasury in 1717 of those which he examined makes their values, as follows:

	Penny-weights.	Grains.	Containing grains of pure silver.
The Seville piece of eight	17	12	387
The Mexico piece of eight	17	$10\frac{3}{4}$	$385\frac{1}{2}$
The Pillar piece of eight	17	9	$385\frac{3}{4}$
The new Seville piece of eight	14	....	$308\frac{7}{10}$

The financier states the old dollar as containing 376 grains of fine silver and the new 365 grains. If the dollars circulating among us be of every date equally, we should examine the quantity of pure metal in each and from them form an average for our Unit. This is a work proper to be committed to Mathematicians as well as merchants and which should be decided on actual and accurate experiment.

The quantum of alloy is also to be decided. Some is necessary to prevent the coin from wearing too fast. Too much fills our pockets with coppers instead of silver. The silver coins assayed by Sir Isaac Newton varied from $1\frac{1}{2}$ to 76 pennyweight alloy in the pound troy of mixed metal. The British standard has 18 dwt. The Spanish coins assayed by Sir Isaac Newton have from 18 to $19\frac{1}{2}$ dwt. The new French crown has in fact $19\frac{1}{2}$, though by edict it should have 20 dwt, that is $\frac{1}{12}$. The taste of our countrymen will require that the [their] furniture plate should be as good as the British standard. Taste cannot be controuled by law. Let it then give the law in a point, which is indifferent to a certain degree. Let the Legislatures fix the alloys of furniture plate at 18 dwt. the British standard, and Congress that of their coin at one ounce in the pound, the French standard. This proportion has been found convenient for the alloy of gold coin and it will simplify the system of our mint to alloy both metals in the same degree. [The coin too being the least pure will be less easily melted into plate.] These reasons are light indeed and of course will only weigh, if no heavier ones can be opposed to them.

The proportion between the values of gold and silver is a mercantile problem altogether. It would be inaccurate to fix it by the popular exchanges of a half Joe for eight dollars, a Louis for 4 French crowns or five Louis for 23 dollars. The first of these would be to adopt the Spanish proportion between gold and silver; the second the French, the third a mere popular barter, wherein convenience is consulted more than accuracy. The legal proportion in Spain is 16 for 1, in England 15½ for 1, in France [uncertain in the U. S. in the printed copy,] 15 for 1. The Spaniards and English are found in experience to retain an over proportion of gold coins and to lose their silver. The French have a greater proportion of silver. The difference at market has been on the decrease. The financier states it at present at 14½ for 1.

Just principles will lead us to disregard legal proportions altogether; to enquire into the market price of gold in the several countries with which we shall principally be connected in commerce, and to take an average from them. Perhaps we might with safety lean to a proportion somewhat above par for gold, considering our neighbourhood and commerce with the sources of the coins and the tendency which the high price of gold in Spain has to draw thither all that of their mines, leaving silver principally for our and other markets. It is not impossible that 15 for 1 may be found an eligible proportion. I state it however as conjectural only.

As to the alloy of gold coin, the British is an ounce in the pound; the French, Spanish and Portuguese differ from that only from ¼ of a gram [to a grain] and a half. I should therefore prefer the British, merely because its fraction stands in a more simple form and facilitates the calculations into which it enters.

Should the unit be fixed at 365 grains of pure silver, gold at 15 for 1, and the alloy of both be one-twelfth the weight of the coins will be as follows:

	Grains.		Grains.		Dwt.	Grs.
The gold piece cont'g..	243⅓	pure metal	22.12	of alloy will weigh	11:	.145
The unit or dollar......	365	"	33.18	"	16:	14.18
*The half doll. or 5-tents	182½	"	16.59	"	8:	7.09
The fifth or pistreen....	73	"	6.63	"	3:	7.63
The tenth or bit......	36½	"	3.318	"	1:	15.818
The twentieth or half-bit	18¼	"	1.659	"		19.9

The quantity of fine silver which shall constitute the unit being settled and the proportion of the value of gold to that of silver; a table should be formed from the assay before suggested, classing the several foreign coins according to their fineness, declaring the worth of a pennyweight or grain in each class and that they shall be lawful tender at those rates if not clipped or otherwise diminished, and where diminished offering their value for them at the mint, deducting the expense

---

*This is omitted in the printed copy.

of recoinage. Here the legislatures should co-operate with Congress in providing that no money be received or paid at their treasuries or by any of their officers or any bank but on actual weight; in making it criminal in a high degree to deminish their own coins and in some smaller degree to offer them in payment when diminished.

That this subject may be properly prepared and in readiness for Congress to take up at their meeting in November, something must now be done. The present session drawing to a close they probably would not choose to enter far into this undertaking themselves. The Committee of the States however, during the recess, will have time to digest it thoroughly, if Congress will fix some general principles for their government.

Suppose then they]be instructed—

To appoint proper persons to assay and examine with the utmost accuracy practicable the Spanish milled dollars of different dates in circulation with us.

To assay and examine in like manner the fineness of all the other coins which may be found in circulation within these states.

To receive and lay before Congress the reports on the result of these assays.

To appoint also proper persons to inquire what are the proportions between the values of fine gold and fine silver at the markets, of the several countries with which we are or probably may be connected in commerce and what would be the proper proportion here, having regard to the average of their values at those markets and to other circumstances and to report the same to the Committee to be by them laid before Congress.

To prepare an Ordinance for establishing the Unit of money within these states; for subdividing it and for striking coins of gold, silver and copper on the following principles,

That the money Unit of these states shall be equal in value to a Spanish milled dollar containing so much fine silver as the assay before directed shall show to be contained, on an average in dollars of the several dates circulating with us.

That this Unit shall be divided into tenths and hundredths.

That there shall be a coin of silver of the value of an unit. One other of the same metal of the value of one tenth of an unit. One other of copper of the value of the hundredth of an unit. That there shall be a coin of gold of the value of ten Units, according to the report before directed and the judgment of the Committee thereon.

That the alloy of the said coins of gold and silver shall be equal in weight to one-eleventh part of the fine metal.

That there be proper devices for these coins.

That measures be proposed for preventing their diminution and also their currency and that of any others when diminished.

That the several foreign coins be described and classed in the said ordinance, the fineness of each class stated and its value by weight estimated in Units and decimal parts of an Unit, and that the said draught of an Ordinance be reported to Congress at their next meeting for their consideration and determination.

The proposals of Morris and Jefferson were, however, not

carried into effect, and the matter remained in this unsettled state until May 13, 1785, when the Grand Committee on the Money Unit made its report. That report is couched in the following terms:

REPORT OF A GRAND COMMITTEE ON THE MONEY UNIT.
1785.

[From MS. Reports of the Committee on Finance of Continental Congress, volume 26, pages 537-560.]

PROPOSITIONS RESPECTING THE COINAGE OF GOLD, SILVER AND COPPER.

1st. The value of Silver compared with Gold,
2d. The weight or size of the several pieces of money that are to be made,
3d. The Money Arithmetic or the mode in which it is to be counted, and
4th. The Charges of Coinage are to be considered.

1. In France 1 grain of pure Gold is counted worth 15 grains of silver. In Spain 16 grains of silver are exchanged for 1 of Gold and in England 15½th. In both of the Kingdoms last mentioned Gold is the prevailing money, because Silver is undervalued. In France Silver prevails. Sundry advantages would arise to us from a system by which silver might become the prevailing money. This would operate as a bounty to draw it from our neighbors by whom it is not sufficiently esteemed. Silver is not exported as easily as gold and it is a more useful metal.

Certainly our Exchange should not be more than 15 gr. of silver for 1 of Gold. It has been alleged by the late Financier that we should not give more than 14½. Perhaps 14¾ would be a better medium considering the quality of Gold that may be expected from Portugal.

2. The weight, size or value of the several pieces of money that shall be made or rather the most convenient value of the money unit is a question not easily determined considering that most of the citizens of the U. S. are accustomed to count in Pounds, Shillings and Pence and that those sums are of different values in the different states, hence they convey no distinct ideas. The money of the U. S. should be equally fitted to all. The late Financier has proposed to make gold and silver Pieces of particular weight, and there is a very simple process by which the imaginary money of the several States may be translated into such pieces or vice versa. He proposes that the Money Unit be one-quarter of a grain of pure silver; that the smallest coin be of Copper which shall be worth five of those Units. The smallest silver coin to be worth 100 units, another to be worth 500, and another of 1000 and thus increasing decimally.

The objections to this plan are that it introduces a coin unlike in value to anything now in use; It departs from the national mode of keeping accounts, and tends to preserve inconvenient prejudices whence it must prevent national uniformity in accounts; a thing greatly to be desired.

Another plan has been offered, which proposes that the money unit be one dollar; and the smallest coin is to be of copper, of which 200 shall pass for one dollar. This plan also proposes, that the several pieces shall increase in a decimal ratio; and that all accounts be kept in decimals, which is certainly by much the most short and simple mode.

In favor of this plan it is urged, that a dollar, the proposed unit, has long been in general use; its value is familiar. This accords with the national mode of keeping accounts, and may in time produce the happy effect of uniformity in counting money throughout the Union.

3. The money Arithmetic, though an important question, is one that can admit of little dispute. All accomptants must prefer decimals.

4. What is the best mode of defraying the expense of coinage? Different nations have adopted different systems. The British value their Silver when coined, no higher than Bullion; Hence it follows that the expense of the mint, increasing the civil list, must be paid by a general tax; and tradesmen are disposed to work up the current coin, by which the tax is increased and continued. In some other countries Silver or Gold when coined, are valued above the price of Bullion; whence tradesmen are discouraged from melting or working up the current coin, and the mint is rather profitable than burdensome. Certainly there are good and conclusive reasons, why we should value the national coin above the price of Bullion; but there is a certain point beyond which we may not proceed, lest we encourage counterfeits or private imitations of our coin. It has been proposed to make a difference of $2\frac{1}{2}$ per cent. nearly as an allowance for the Coinage of Gold and of 3.013 per cent. for the coinage of silver. It is probable that 3 per cent. would more than defray the expense of coining silver, in which case it would be a temptation to private imitation and would operate against the free circulation of the money as being valued too high. It is to be remembered that silver coin ought to be encouraged and probably 2 per cent. or $2\frac{1}{2}$ per cent. would be a proper difference between silver coined and Bullion; The same difference to be made in the price of Gold. If this does not fully pay the expenses of the mint there will be a much larger gain on the coinage of copper, and if there should remain a small balance against the mint its operation will not be unfavorable.

The Coinage of Copper is a subject that claims our immediate attention. From the small value of the several pieces of copper coin this medium of exchange has been too much neglected. The more valuable metals are daily giving place to base British half-pence and no means are used to prevent the fraud. This disease which is neglected in the beginning because it appears trifling may finally prove very destructive to commerce. It is admitted that Copper may at this instant be purchased in America at $\frac{1}{6}$ of a Dlr. a pound. British half-pence made at the Tower are 48 to the pound. Those manufactured at Birmingham and shipped in thousands for our use are much lighter and they are of base metal, it can hardly be said that 72 of them are worth a pound of copper. Hence it will follow that we give for British half-pence about six times their value. There are no materials from which we can estimate the weight of half-pence that have been imported from Britain since the late war, but we have heard of sundry shipments being ordered, to the nominal amount of 1,000 guineas, and we are told that no Packet arrives from England by which we are not accommodated with some hundred weight of base half-pence. It is a very moderate computation which states our loss on the last twelve months at 30 thousand dollars by the commerce of vile coin. The whole expense of a mint would not have amounted to half of that sum, and the whole expense of domestic coinage would remain in the country.

The following forms of money are submitted:

	Dlrs.
1 Piece of Gold of...	5.
1 Do of Silver of	1*
1 Do	½ or .5
1 Do...	¼ or .25
1 Do...	$\frac{1}{10}$ or .1
1 Do...	$\frac{1}{20}$ or .05
1 Piece of copper of...	$\frac{1}{100}$ or .01
1 Do..	$\frac{1}{200}$ or .005.

The quantity of pure silver being fixed that is to be in the Unit or Dlr and the relation between Silver and Gold being fixed, all the other weights must follow. When it is considered that the Spaniards have been reducing the weight of their Dlrs, and that instead of 385, the grains of pure silver in the old Mexican dollar, the new dollars have not more than 365 grains, it will hardly be thought that 362 grains of pure silver is too little for the federal coin which is to be current in all payments for one dollar.

Some of the old Dlrs will admit of a second coinage, but the new ones will not. If the value of Gold compared to that of silver be fixed at 15 to one, and the alloy in each be $\frac{1}{12}$th, the weight of the several denominations will be readily determined. The price of bullion is immediately determined by the percentage that is charged towards the expenses of the mint. If the United States shall determine to adhere to the dollar as their money of account, and to simplify accounts by the use of decimals, there is nothing to prevent the immediate commencement of a coinage of copper.

Let the copper pieces, of which 100 are to pass for a Dlr, contain each 131 grains of pure copper, or 44 of them weigh 1 Pound. In this case our copper coin, when compared with the money of accot., will be 6 per cent. better than that of Great Britain. There will remain a sufficient profit on the coinage.

Copper of the best quality in plates may be purchased in Europe at 10*d.* ½ stg. In cutting blanks there will be a waste of 22 per cent. Those clippings are worth 7*d.* ½ p. lb. Thence the blanks will cost 11*d.* ½ nearly; it may be stated at 1*s.* 9*d.*, New York money p. pound, exclusive of the expense of cutting them, which is not great, as one man can readily cut 100 weight in a day.

The operation, improperly called milling, by which the sharp edges are worn off from the coppers, is not more expensive than cutting the blanks. In the process of coining Copper, eight artists or labourers may be required. One Engraver, 1 Labourer for the blank press, One Smith, 5 Labourers for the Coining Press.

By those people 100 weight of copper may readily be coined every day, or the value of 44 Dlrs. Deducting the necessary expenses, there may be saved 30 per cent.

---

* Containing 362 gr. pure silver. This is the Unit or money of account.

It will be noticed that the report of the Grand Committee on the Money Unit contends that exchange in the United States should not be more than 15 grains of silver for 1 of gold; that the charge for coinage should be 2½ per cent. for gold and a little over 3 per cent. for silver; that the unit should be a dollar of 362 grains of pure silver with a multiple gold piece of 5 dollars and decimal aliquot parts.

On July 6, 1785, the Congress adopted the silver dollar as the currency basis on a decimal system, but no mint was established, although the country was suffering great loss in consequence of the circulation of base copper coins made in Birmingham.

REPORT OF THE BOARD OF TREASURY.

On April 8, 1786, the Board of Treasury made a report in triplicate to the President of Congress, and although they mentioned the fact that the ratio then prevailing in the country was 1 : 15.60, their report shows the following adjustment of the coins:

	Weight of—		Ratio between silver and gold coins.
	Silver dollar.	Gold dollar.	
	Grains fine.	*Grains fine.*	
Report, form No. 1...............	375.64	24.6268	1 : 15.253
Report, form No. 2...............	350.09	23.79	1 : 14.749
Report, form No. 3...............	521.73	34.782	1 : 15

The first form of the report was followed in accordance with a resolution passed on the 8th of August, 1786, and on the 16th of October following the ordinance for the establishment of the mint of the United States of America and for regulating the value of coin passed Congress.

The resolution of August 8, 1786, fixed the mint price of the pound troy, of gold at 209 dollars, 7 dimes, 7 cents, and 7 mills; and of silver at 13 dollars, 7 dimes, 7 cents, and 7 mills. The mint charge was about 2 per cent. on silver and gold, "bringing the ratio on bullion at the mint to 15.22, a little below the ratio in the coin."

THE SILVER PERIOD, 1792–1834—ACT OF APRIL 2, 1792.

None of the regulations of Congress were put in force for a number of years, and the matter was not again brought before Congress until the report of Alexander Hamilton, Secretary of the Treasury, dated January 28, 1791, was laid before the House of Representatives. This very remarkable and statesmanlike paper is here given in full:

REPORT OF ALEXANDER HAMILTON ON THE ESTABLISHMENT OF A MINT.

[In the House of Representatives of the United States, Saturday, February 5, 1791.]
[Extract from the Journal.]

On motion,

Ordered, That the report of the Secretary of the Treasury, relatively to the establishment of a mint, which was made to this House on Friday, the 28th ultimo, be sent to the Senate for their information.

JOHN BECKLEY, *Clerk.*

The Secretary of the Treasury having attentively considered the subject referred to him by the order of the House of Representatives, of the fifteenth day of April last, relative to the establishment of a Mint, most respectfully submits the result of his inquiries and reflections.

A plan for an establishment of this nature, involves a great variety of considerations, intricate, nice, and important. The general state of debtor and creditor; all the relations and consequences of price; the essential interests of trade and industry; the value of all property; the whole income, both of the State and of individuals, are liable to be sensibly influenced, beneficially or otherwise, by the judicious or injudicious regulation of this interesting object.

It is one, likewise, not more necessary than difficult to be rightly adjusted; one which has frequently occupied the reflections and researches of politicians, without having harmonized their opinions on some of the most important of the principles which enter into its discussion. Accordingly, different systems continue to be advocated, and the systems of different nations, after much investigation, continue to differ from each other.

But if a right adjustment of the matter be truly of such nicety and difficulty, a question naturally arises, whether it may not be most advisable to leave things in this respect, in the state in which they are? Why, might it be asked, since they have so long proceeded in a train which has caused no general sensation of inconvenience, should alterations be attempted, the precise effect of which cannot with certainty be calculated?

The answer to this question is not perplexing. The immense disorder which actually reigns in so delicate and important a concern, and the still greater disorder which is every moment possible, call loudly for a reform. The dollar originally contemplated in the money transactions of this country, by successive diminutions of its weight and fineness, has sustained a depreciation of five per cent.; and yet the new dollar has a currency in all payments in place of the old, with scarcely any attention to the difference between them. The operation of this in depreciating the value of property depending upon past contracts, and (as far as inattention to the alteration in the coin may be supposed to leave prices stationary) of all other property, is apparent. Nor can it require argument to prove that a nation ought not to suffer the value of the property of its citizens to fluctuate with the fluctuations of a foreign mint, and to change with the changes in the regulations of a foreign sovereign. This, nevertheless, is the condition of one which, having no coins of its own, adopts with implicit confidence those of other countries.

The unequal values allowed, in different parts of the Union, to coins of the same intrinsic worth; the defective species of them which embarrass the circulation of some of the States; and the dissimilarity in their several moneys of account, are inconveniences which, if not to be ascribed to the want of a national coinage, will at least be most effectually remedied by the establishment of one: a measure that will, at the same time, give additional security against impositions by counterfeit as well as by base currencies.

It was with great reason, therefore, that the attention of Congress, under the late Confederation, was repeatedly drawn to the establishment of a mint; and it is with equal reason that the subject has been resumed, now that the favorable change which has taken taken place in the situation of public affairs admits of its being carried into execution.

But, though the difficulty of devising a proper establishment ought not to deter from undertaking so necessary a work, yet it cannot but inspire diffidence in one, whose duty it is made to propose a plan for the purpose, and may perhaps be permitted to be relied upon as some excuse for any errors which may be chargeable upon it, or for any deviations from sounder principles which may have been suggested by others, or even in part acted upon by the former Government of the United States.

In order to a right judgment of what ought to be done, the following particulars require to be discussed:

1st. What ought to be the nature of the money unit of the United States?

2d. What the proportion between gold and silver, if coins of both metals are to be established?

3d. What the proportion and composition of alloy in each kind?

4th. Whether the expense of coinage shall be defrayed by the Government, or out of the material itself?

5th. What shall be the number, denomination, sizes, and devices of the coins?

6th. Whether foreign coins shall be permitted to be current or not; if the former, at what rate, and for what period?

THE MONEY UNIT.

A prerequisite to determining with propriety what ought to be the money unit of the United States, is to endeavor to form as accurate an idea as the nature of the case will admit of what it actually is. The pound, though of various value, is the unit in the money of account of all the States. But it is not equally easy to pronounce what is to be considered as the unit in the coins. There being no formal regulation on the point (the resolutions of Congress of the 6th July, 1785, and 8th of August, 1786, having never yet been carried into operation), it can only be inferred from usage or practice. The manner of adjusting foreign exchanges would seem to indicate the dollar as best entitled to that character. In these, the old piaster of Spain, or old Seville piece of eight *rials*, of the value of four shillings and six-pence sterling, is evidently contemplated. The computed par between Great Britain and Pennsylvania, will serve as an example. According to that, one hundred pounds sterling is equal to one hundred and sixty-six pounds and two-thirds of a pound Pennsylvania currency; which corresponds with the proportion between 4*s.* 6*d.* sterling and 7*s.* 6*d.*, the current value of the dollar in that State, by invariable usage. And, as far as the information of the Secretary goes, the same comparison holds in the other States.

But this circumstance in favor of the dollar, loses much of its weight from two considerations. That species of coin has never had any settled or standard value, according to weight or fineness, but has been permitted to circulate by tale, without regard to either, very much as mere money of convenience, while gold has had a fixed price by weight, and with an eye to its fineness. This greater stability of value of the gold coins, is an argument of force for regarding the money unit as having been hitherto virtually attached to gold, rather than to silver.

Twenty-four grains and six-eighths of a grain of fine gold, have corresponded with the nominal value of the dollar in the several States, without regard to the successive diminutions of its intrinsic worth.

But if the dollar should, notwithstanding, be supposed to have the best title to being considered as the present unit in the coins, it would remain to determine what kind of a dollar ought to be understood; or, in other words, what precise quantity of fine silver.

The old piaster of Spain, which appears to have regulated our foreign exchanges, weighed 17 dwt. 12 grains, and contained 386 grains and 15 mites of fine silver. But this piece has been long since out of circulation. The dollars now in common currency are of recent date, and much inferior to that, both in weight and fineness. The average weight of them, upon different trials, in large masses, has been found to be 17 dwt. 8 grains. Their fineness is less precisely ascertained; the results of various assays made by different persons, under the direction of the late Superintendent of the Finances, and of the Secretary, being as various as the assays themselves. The difference between their extremes is not less than 24 grains in a dollar of the same weight and age; which is too much for any probable differences in the pieces. It is rather to be presumed, that a degree of inaccuracy has been occasioned by the want of proper apparatus, and, in general, of practice. The experiment which appears to have the best pretentions to exactness, would make the new dollar to contain 370 grains and 933 thousandth parts of a grain of pure silver.

According to an authority on which the Secretary places reliance, the standard of Spain for its silver coin, in the year 1761, was 261 parts fine and 27 parts alloy; at which proportion, a dollar of 17 dwt. 8 grains, would consist of 377 grains of fine silver, and 39 grains of alloy. But there is no question that this standard has been since altered considerably for the worse: to what precise point, is not as well ascertained as could be wished; but, from a computation of the value of dollars in the markets both of Amsterdam and London (a criterion which cannot materially mislead,) the new dollar appears to contain about 368 grains of fine silver, and that which immediately preceded it about 374 grains.

In this state of things, there is some difficulty in defining the dollar, which is to be understood as constituting the present money unit, on the supposition of its being most applicable to that species of coin. The old Seville piece of 386 grains and 15 mites fine, comports best with the computations of foreign exchanges, and with the more ancient contracts respecting landed property; but far the greater number of contracts still in operation concerning that kind of property, and all those of a merely personal nature, now in force, must be referred to a dollar of a different kind. The actual dollar at the time of contracting, is the only one which can be supposed to have been intended; and it has been seen that, as long ago as the year 1761, there had been a material degradation of the standard. And even in regard to the more ancient contracts, no person has ever had any idea of a scruple about receiving the dollar of the day as a full equivalent for the nominal sum which the dollar originally imported.

A recurrence, therefore, to the ancient dollar, would be in the greatest number of cases an innovation *in fact*, and in all, an innovation in respect to opinion. The actual dollar in common circulation has evidently a much better claim to be regarded as the actual money unit.

The mean intrinsic value of the different kinds of known dollars has been intimated as affording the proper criterion. But when it is recollected that the more ancient and more valuable ones are not now to be met with at all in circulation, and that the mass of those generally current is composed of the newest and most inferior kinds, it will be perceived that even an equation of that nature would be a considerable innovation upon the real present state of things; which it will certainly be prudent to approach, as far as may be consistent with the permanent order designed to be introduced.

An additiontal reason for considering the prevailing dollar as the standard of the present money unit, rather than the the ancient one, is, that it will be not only be conformable to the true existing proportion between the two metals in this country, but will be more conformable to that which obtains in the commercial world generally.

The difference established by custom in the United States between coined gold and coined silver has been stated upon another occasion to be nearly as 1 to 15.6. This, if truly the case, would imply that gold was extremely overvalued in the United States; for the highest *actual proportion*, in any part of Europe, very little, if at all, exceeds 1 to 15; and the average proportion throughout Europe is probably not more than about 1 to 14.8. But that statement has proceeded upon the idea of the ancient dollar. One pennyweight of gold of twenty-two carats fine, at

6s. 8d., and the old Seville piece of 386 grains and 15 mites of pure silver, at 7s. 6d., furnish the exact ratio of 1 to 15.6262. But this does not coincide with the real difference between the metals in our market, or, which is with us the same thing, in our currency. To determine this, the quantity of fine silver in the general mass of the dollars now in circulation must afford the rule. Taking the rate of the late dollar of 374 grains, the proportion would be as 1 to 15.11. Taking the rate of the newest dollar, the proportion would be as 1 to 14.87. The mean of the two would give the proportion of 1 to 15, very nearly; less than the legal proportion in the coins of Great Britain, which is as 1 to 15.2; but somewhat more than the actual or market proportion, which is not quite 1 to 15.

The preceding view of the subject does not indeed furnish a precise or certain definition of the present unit in the coins, but it furnishes data which will serve as guides in the progress of the investigation. It ascertains, at least, that the sum in the money of account of each State, corresponding with the nominal value of the dollar in such State, corresponds also with 24 grains and ⅞ of a grain of fine gold; and with something between 368 and 374 grains of fine silver.

The Unit should be attached to both Gold and Silver.

The next inquiry towards a right determination of what ought to be the future money unit of the United States, turns upon these questions: Whether it ought to be peculiarly attached to either of these metals, in preference to the other or not? and, if to either, to which of them?

The suggestions and proceedings hitherto have had for their object the annexing of it emphatically to the silver dollar. A resolution of Congress of the 6th of July, 1785, declares that the money unit of the United States shall be a dollar; and another resolution of the 8th of August, 1786, fixes that dollar at 375 grains and 64 hundredths of a grain of fine silver. The same resolution, however, determines that there shall also be two gold coins: one of 246 grains and 268 parts of a grain of pure gold, equal to ten dollars; and the other, of one half that quantity of pure gold, equal to five dollars. And it is not explained whether either of the two species of coins, of gold or silver, shall have any greater legality in payments than the other. Yet it would seem that a preference in this particular is necessary to execute the idea of attaching the unit exclusively to one kind. If each of them be as valid as the other, in payments to any amount, it is not obvious in what effectual sense either of them can be deemed the money unit, rather than the other.

If the general declaration, that the dollar shall be the money unit of the United States could be understood to give it a superior legality in payments, the institution of coins of gold, and the declaration that each of them shall be *equal* to a certain number of dollars, would appear to destroy that inference. And the circumstance of making the dollar the unit in the money of account, seems to be rather matter of form than circumstance.

Contrary to the ideas which have heretofore prevailed, in the suggestions concerning a coinage for the United States, though not without much hesitation, arising from a deference for those ideas, the Secretary is, upon the whole, strongly inclined to the opinion, that a preference ought to be given to neither of the metals for the money unit. Perhaps, if either were to be preferred, it ought to be gold rather than silver.

The reasons are these:

The inducement to such a preference is, to render the unit as little variable as possible; because on this depends the steady value of all contracts, and, in a certain sense, of all other property. And it is truly observed, that if the unit belong indiscriminately to both the metals, it is subject to all the fluctuations that happen in the relative value which they bear to each other. But the same reason would lead to annexing it to that particular one, which is itself the least liable to variation; if there be, in this respect, any discernible difference between the two.

Gold may, perhaps, in certain senses, be said to have greater stability than silver; as, being of superior value, less liberties have been taken with it, in the regulations of different countries. Its standard has remained more uniform, and it has, in other respects, undergone fewer changes; as, being not so much an article of merchandise, owing to the use made of silver in the trade with the East Indies and China, it is less liable to be influenced by circumstances of commercial demand. And if, reasoning by analogy, it could be affirmed, that there is a physical probability of greater proportional increase in the quantity of silver than in that of gold, it would afford an additional reason for calculating on greater steadiness in the value of the latter.

As long as gold, either from its intrinsic superiority as a metal, from its greater rarity, or from the prejudices of mankind, retains so considerable a pre-eminence in value over silver, as it has hitherto had, a natural consequence of this seems to be that its condition will be more stationary. The revolutions, therefore, which may take place in the comparative value of gold and silver, will be changes in the state of the latter, rather than in that of the former.

If there should be an appearance of too much abstraction in any of these ideas, it may be remarked, that the first and most simple impressions do not naturally incline to giving a preference to the inferior or least valuable of the two metals.

It is sometimes observed, that silver ought to be encouraged rather than gold, as being more conducive to the extension of bank circulation, from the greater difficulty and inconvenience which its greater bulk, compared with its value, occasiohs in the transportation of it. But the bank circulation is desirable, rather as *an auxiliary to*, than as *a substitute for* that of the precious metals, and ought to be left to its natural course. Artificial expedients to extend it, by opposing obstacles to the other, are at least not recommended by any very obvious advantages. And, in general, it is the safest rule to regulate every particular institution or object, according to the principles which, in relation to itself, appear the most sound. In addition to this, it may be observed, that the inconvenience of transporting either of the metals, is sufficiently great to induce a preference of bank paper, whenever it can be made to answer the purpose equally well.

But, upon the whole, it seems to be most adviseable, as has been observed, not to attach the unit exclusively to either of the metals; because this cannot be done effectually, without destroying the office and character of one of them as money, and reducing it to the situation of a mere merchandise; which, accordingly, at different times, has been proposed from different and very respectable quarters;

but which would probably be a greater evil than occasional variations in the unit, from the fluctuations in the relative value of the metals; especially if care be taken to regulate the proportion between them, with an eye to their average commercial value.

To annul the use of either of the metals, as money, is to abridge the quantity of circulating medium; and is liable to all the objections which arise from a comparison of the benefits of a full, with the evils of a scanty circulation.

It is not a satisfactory answer to say, that none but the favored metal would in this case find its way into the country, as in that all balances must be paid. The practicability of this would, in some measure, depend on the abundance or scarcity of it in the country paying. Where there was but little, it either would not be procurable at all, or it would cost a premium to obtain it; which, in every case of a competition with others, in a branch of trade, would constitute a deduction from the profits of the party receiving. Perhaps, too, the embarrassment which such a circumstance might sometimes create, in the pecuniary liquidation of balances, might lead to additional efforts to find a substitute in commodities, and might so far impede the introduction of the metals. Neither could the exclusion of either of them be deemed, in other respects, favorable to commerce. It is often, in the course of trade, as desirable to possess the kind of money, as the kind of commodities best adopted to a foreign market.

It seems, however, most probable, that the chief, if not the sole, effect of such a regulation, whoul be to diminish the utility of one of the metals. It could hardly prove an obstacle to the introduction of that which was excluded in the natural course of trade, because it would always command a ready sale for the purpose of exportation to foreign markets. But such an effect, if the only one, is not to be regarded as a trivial inconvenience.

THE COINAGE RATIO OF THE TWO METALS SHOULD BE THEIR MARKET OR COMMERCIAL RATIO.

If, then, the unit ought not to be attached exclusively to either of the metals, the proportion which ought to subsist between them, in the coins, becomes a preliminary inquiry, in order to its proper adjustment. This proportion appears to be, in several views, of no inconsiderable moment.

One consequence of overvaluing either metal, in respect to the other, is the banishment of that which is undervalued. If two countries are supposed, in one of which the proportion of gold to silver is as 1 to 16, in the other as 1 to 15, gold being worth more, silver less, in one than in the other, it is manifest that, in their reciprocal payments, each will select that species which it values least, to pay to the other where it is valued most. Besides this, the dealers in money will, from the same cause, often find a profitable traffic in an exchange of the metals between the two countries. And hence it would come to pass, if other things were equal, that the greatest part of the gold would be collected in one, and the greatest part of the silver in the other. The course of trade might in some degree counteract the tendency of the difference in the legal proportions by the market value; but this is so far and so often influenced by the legal rates, that it does not prevent their producing the effect which is inferred. Facts, too, verify the inference. In Spain and England, where gold is rated higher than in other parts of Europe, there is a scarcity of silver; while it is found to abound in France and Holland, where it is rated higher in proportion to gold than in the neighboring nations. And it is continually flowing from Europe to China and the East Indies, owing to the comparative cheapness of it in the former, and the dearness of it in the latter.

This consequence is deemed by some not very material; and there are even persons who, from a fanciful predilection to gold, are willing to invite it, even by a higher price. But general utility will best be promoted by a due proportion of both metals. If gold be most convenient in large payments, silver is best adapted to the more minute and ordinary circulation.

But it is to be suspected that there is another consequence, more serious than the one which has been mentioned. This is the diminution of the total quantity of specie which a country would naturally possess.

It is evident that as often as a country, which overrates either of the metals, receive a payment in that metal, it gets a less actual quantity than it ought to do, or than it would do, if the rate were a just one.

It is also equally evident, that there will be a continual effort to make payment to it in that species to which it has annexed an exaggerated estimation, wherever it is current at a less proportional value. And it would seem to be a very natural effect of these two causes, not only that the mass of the precious metals in the country in question would consist chiefly of that kind to which it had given an extraordinary *value*, but that it would be absolutely less than if they had been duly proportioned to each other.

A conclusion of this sort, however, is to be drawn with great caution. In such matters, there are always some local and many other particular circumstances, which qualify and vary the operation of general principles, even where they are just; and there are endless combinations, very difficult to be analyzed, which often render principles, that have the most plausible pretensions, unsound and delusive.

There ought, for instance, according to those which have been stated, to have been formerly a greater quantity of gold in proportion to silver in the United States, than there has been; because the actual value of gold in the country, compared with silver, was perhaps higher than in any other. But our situation with regard to the West India islands, into some of which there is a large influx of silver directly from the mines of South America, occasions an extraordinary supply of that metal, and consequently a greater proportion of it in our circulation than might have been expected from its relative value.

What influence the proportion under consideration may have upon the state of prices, and how far this may counteract its tendency to increase or lessen the quantity of the metals, are points not easy to be developed; and yet they are very necessary to an accurate judgment of the true operation of the thing.

But however impossible it may be to pronounce with certainty, that the possession of a less quantity of specie is a consequence of overvaluing either of the metals, there is enough of probability in the considerations which seem to indicate it, to form an argument of weight against such overvaluations.

MONETARY LEGISLATION.

A third ill consequence resulting from it is, a greater and more frequent disturbance of the state of the money unit, by a greater and more frequent diversity between the legal and marked proportions of the metals. This has not hitherto been experienced in the United States, but it has been experienced elsewhere; and from its not having been felt by us hitherto, it does not follow that this will not be the case hereafter, when our commerce shall have attained a maturity which will place it under the influence of more fixed principles.

In establishing a proportion between the metals, there seems to be an option of one of two things—

To approach, as nearly as can be ascertained, the mean or average proportion, in what may be called the commercial world; or,

To retain that which now exists in the United States. As far as these happen to coincide, they will render the course to be pursued more plain and more certain.

To ascertain the first, with precision, would require better materials than are possessed, or than could be obtained, without an inconvenient delay.

Sir Isaac Newton, in a representation to the Treasury of Great Britain, in the year 1717, after stating the particular proportions in the different countries of Europe, concludes thus: "By the course of trade and exchange between nation and nation, in all Europe, fine gold is to fine silver as $14\frac{3}{4}$, or 15 to 1."

But however accurate and decisive this authority may be deemed, in relation to the period to which it applies, it cannot be taken, at the distance of more than seventy years, as a rule for determining the existing proportion. Alterations have been since made, in the regulations of their coins by several nations; which, as well as the course of trade, have an influence upon the market values. Nevertheless, there is reason to believe, that the state of the matter, as represented by Sir Isaac Newton, is not very remote from its actual state.

In Holland, the greatest *money* market of Europe, gold was to silver, in December, 1789, as 1 to 14.88; and in that of London it has been, for some time past, but little different, approaching perhaps something nearer 1 to 15.

It has been seen that the existing proportion between the two metals in this country is about 1 to 15.

It is fortunate, in this respect, that the innovations of the Spanish mint have imperceptibly introduced a proportion so analogous as this is to that which prevails among the principal commercial nations, as it greatly facilitates a proper regulation of the matter.

This proportion of 1 to 15 is recommended by the particular situation of our trade, as being very nearly that which obtains in the market of Great Britain; to which nation our specie is principally exported. A lower rate for either of the metals in our market, as in hers, might not only afford a motive the more in certain cases, to remit in specie rather than in commodities; but it might, in some others, cause us to pay a greater quantity of it for a given sum than we should otherwise do. If the effect should rather be to occasion a premium to be given for the metal which was underrated, this would obviate those disadvantages; but it would involve another, a customary difference between the market and legal proportions, which would amount to a species of disorder in the national coinage.

Looking forward to the payments of interest hereafter to be made to Holland, the same proportion does not appear ineligible. The present legal proportion in the coins of Holland is stated at 1 to $14\frac{9}{10}$. That of the market varies somewhat at different times, but seldom very widely from this point.

There can hardly be a better rule in any country for the legal, than the market proportion, if this can be supposed to have been produced by the free and steady course of commercial principles. The presumption in such case is, that each metal finds its true level, according to its intrinsic utility, in the general system of money operations.

But it must be admitted that this argument in favor of continuing the existing proportion is not applicable to the state of the coins with us. There have been too many artificial and heterogeneous ingredients—too much want of order in the pecuniary transactions of this country—to authorize the attributing the effects which have appeared to the regular operations of commerce. A proof of this is to be drawn from the alterations which have happened in the proportion between the metals merely by the successive degradations of the dollar, in consequence of the mutability of a foreign mint. The value of gold to silver appears to have declined, wholly from this cause, from $15\frac{6}{10}$ to about 15 to 1; yet, as this last proportion, however produced, coincides so nearly with what may be deemed the commercial average, it may be supposed to furnish as good a rule as can be pursued.

The only question seems to be, whether the value of gold ought not to be a little lowered, to bring it to a more exact level with the two markets which have been mentioned; but, as the ratio of 1 to 15 is so nearly conformable to the state of those markets, and best agrees with that of our own, it will probably be found the most eligible. If the market of Spain continues to give a higher value to gold (as it has done in time past) than that which is recommended, there may be some advantage in a middle station.

THE PROPORTION AND COMPOSITION OF ALLOY IN THE COINS.

A further preliminary to the adjustment of the future money unit is, to determine what shall be the proportion and composition of alloy in each species of the coins.

The first, by the resolution of the 8th of August, 1786, before referred to, is regulated at one-twelfth, or in other words, at 1 part alloy to 11 parts fine, whether gold or silver; which appears to be a convenient rule; unless there should be some collateral consideration which may dictate a departure from it. Its correspondency, in regard to both metals, is a recommendation of it, because a difference could answer no purpose of pecuniary or commercial utility, and uniformity is favorable to order.

This ratio, as it regards gold, coincides with the proportion, real or professed, in the coins of Portugal, England, France and Spain. In those of the two former it is real; in those of the two latter there is a deduction for what is called *remedy of weight and alloy*, which is in the nature of an allowance to the master of the mint for errors and imperfections in the process, rendering the coin either lighter or baser than it ought to be. The same thing is known in the theory of the

English mint, where ⅛ of a carat is allowed. But the difference seems to be, that *there*, it is merely an occasional indemnity within a certain limit, for real and unavoidable errors and imperfections; whereas, in the practice of the mints of France and Spain, it appears to amount to a stated and regular deviation from the nominal standard. Accordingly, the real standards of France and Spain are something worse than 22 carats, or 11 parts in 12 fine.

The principal gold coins in Germany, Holland, Sweden, Denmark, Poland, and Italy, are finer than those of England and Portugal, in different degrees, from 1 carat and ¼ to 1 carat and ⅞, which last is within ⅛ of a carat of pure gold.

There are similar diversities in the standards of the silver coins of the different countries of Europe. That of Great Britain is 222 parts fine, to 18 alloy; those of the other European nations vary from that of Great Britain as widely as from about 17 of the same parts better, to 75 worse.

The principal reasons assigned for the use of alloy, are the saving of expense in the refining of the metals (which in their natural state are usually mixed with a portion of the coarser kinds), and the rendering of them harder as a security against too great waste by friction or wearing. The first reason, drawn from the original composition of the metals, is strengthened at present by the practice of alloying their coins, which has obtained among so many nations. The reality of the effect to which the last reason is applicable, has been denied, and experi- has been appealed to as proving that the more alloyed coins wear faster than the purer. The true state of this matter may be worthy of future investigation, though first appearances are in favor of alloy. In the mean time, the saving of trouble and expense are sufficient inducements to following those examples which suppose its expediency. And the same considerations lead to taking as our models those nations with whom we have most intercourse, and whose coins are most prevalent in our circulation. These are Spain, Portugal, England, and France. The relation which the proposed proportion bears to their gold coins has been explained. In respect to their silver coins, it will not be very remote from the mean of their several standards.

The component ingredients of the alloy in each metal will also require to be regulated. In silver, copper is the only kind in use, and it is doubtless the only proper one. In gold, there is a mixture of silver and copper; in the English coins consisting of equal parts, in the coins of some other countries, varying from ⅓ to ⅔ silver.

The reason of this union of silver with copper is this: The silver counteracts the tendency of the copper to injure the color or beauty of the coin, by giving it too much redness, or rather a coppery hue, which a small quantity will produce; and the copper prevents the too great whiteness which silver alone would confer. It is apprehended that there are considerations which may render it prudent to establish, by law, that the proportion of silver to copper in the gold coins of the United States shall not be more than ½ nor less than ⅓; vesting a discretion in some proper place to regulate the matter within those limits, as experience in the execution may recommend.

WHO SHOULD BEAR THE EXPENSE OF COINAGE?

A third point remains to be discussed, as a prerequisite to the determination of the money unit, which is, whether the expense of coining shall be defrayed by the public, or out of the material itself; or, as it is sometimes stated, whether coinage shall be free, or shall be subject to a duty or imposition? This forms, perhaps, one of the nicest questions in the doctrine of money.

The practice of different nations is dissimilar in this particular. In England, coinage is said to be entirely free; the mint price of the metals in bullion being the same with the value of them in coin. In France, there is a duty, which has been, if it is not now, eight per cent. In Holland, there is a difference between the mint price and the value in the coins, which has been computed at .96, or something less than one per cent. upon gold; at 1.48, or something less than one and a half per cent. upon silver. The resolution of the 8th of August, 1786, proceeds upon the idea of a deduction of a half per cent. from gold, and of two per cent. from silver, as an indemnification for the expense of coining. This is inferred from a report of the late board of treasury, upon which that resolution appears to have been founded.

Upon the supposition that the expense of coinage ought to be defrayed out of the metals, there are two ways in which it may be effected: one, by a reduction of the quantity of fine gold and silver in the coins; the other, by establishing a difference between the value of those metals in the coins, and the mint price of them in bullion.

The first method appears to the Secretary inadmissible. He is unable to distinguish an operation of this sort from that of raising the denomination of the coin; a measure which has been disapproved by the wisest men of the nations in which it has been practised, and condemned by the rest of the world. To declare that a less weight of gold or silver shall pass for the same sum, which before represented a greater weight; or to ordain that the same weight shall pass for a greater sum, are things substantially of one nature. The consequence of either of them, if the change can be realized, is to degrade the money unit; obliging creditors to receive less than their just dues, and depreciating property of every kind; for it is manifest that every thing would, in this case, be represented by a less quantity of gold and silver than before.

It is sometimes observed, on this head, that though any article of property might, in fact, be represented by a less actual quantity of pure metal, it would nevertheless be represented by something of the same intrinsic value. Every fabric, it is remarked, is worth intrinsically the price of the raw material and the expense of fabrication; a truth not less applicable to a piece of coin than to a yard of cloth.

This position, well founded in itself, is here misapplied. It supposes that the coins now in circulation are to be considered as bullion, or, in other words, as a raw material. But the fact is, that the adoption of them as money, has caused them to become the fabric; it has invested them with the character and office of coins, and has given them a sanction and efficacy, equivalent to that of the stamp of the sovereign. The prices of all our commodities, at home and abroad, and of all foreign commodities in our markets, have found their level in conformity to this principle. The foreign coins may be *divested* of the privilege they have hitherto been permitted to enjoy, and may of course be *left* to find their value in the market as a raw material. But the quantity of gold and silver in the national coins, corresponding with a given sum, cannot be made less than heretofore, without disturbing the balance of intrinsic value, and making every acre of land, as well as every bushel of wheat, of less actual worth than in time past. If the United States were isolated, and cut off from all intercourse with the rest of mankind, this reasoning would not be equally conclusive. But it appears decisive, when considered with a view to the relations which commerce has created between us and other countries.

It is, however, not improbable, that the effect meditated would be defeated by a rise of prices proportioned to the diminution of the intrinsic value of the coins. This might be looked for in every enlightened commercial country; but perhaps in none with greater certainty than in this, because in none are men less liable to be the dupes of sounds; in none has authority so little resource for substituting names for things.

A general revolution in prices, though only nominally, and in appearance, could not fail to distract the ideas of the community; and would be apt to breed discontents as well among those who live on the income of their money, as among the poorer classes of the people, to whom the necessaries of life would seem to have become dearer. In the confusion of such a state of things, ideas of value would not improbably adhere to the old coins, which, from that circumstance, instead of feeling the effect of the loss of their privilege as money, would perhaps bear a price in the market relatively to the new ones in exact proportion to their weight. The frequency of the demand of the metals to pay foreign balances, would contribute to this effect.

Among the evils attendant on such an operation, are these: creditors, both of the public and of individuals, would lose a part of their property; public and private credit would receive a wound; the effective revenues of the Government would be diminished. There is scarcely any point in the economy of national affairs, of greater moment than the uniform preservation of the intrinsic value of the money unit. On this the security and steady value of property essentially depend.

The second method, therefore, of defraying the expense of the coinage out of the metals is greatly to be preferred to the other. This is to let the same sum of money continue to represent in the new coins exactly the same quantity of gold and silver as it does in those now current; to allow at the mint such a price only for those metals as will admit of profit just sufficient to satisfy the expense of coinage; to abolish the legal currency of the foreign coins, both in public and private payments; and of course to leave the superior utility of the national coins for domestic purposes, to operate the difference of market value, which is necessary to induce the bringing of bullion to the mint. In this case, all property and labor will still be represented by the same quantity of gold and silver as formerly; and the only change which will be wrought, will consist in annexing the office of money exclusively to the national coins; consequently, withdrawing it from those of foreign countries, and suffering them to become, as they ought to be, mere articles of merchandise.

FOREIGN COINS SHOULD BE TREATED AS MERCHANDISE.

The arguments in favor of a regulation of this kind are: First, That the want of it is a cause of extra expense: there being then no motive of individual interest to distinguish between the national coins and bullion; they are, it is alleged, indiscriminately melted down for domestic manufactures, and exported for the purposes of foreign trade; and it is added, that when the coins become light by wearing, the same quantity of fine gold or silver bears a higher price in bullion than in the coins; in which state of things, the melting down of the coins to be sold as bullion is attended with profit; and from both causes, the expense of the mint, or, in other words, the expense of maintaining the specie capital of the nation, is materially augmented.

Secondly. That the existence of such a regulation promotes a favorable course of exchange, and benefits trade; not only by that circumstance, but by obliging foreigners, in certain cases, to pay dearer for domestic commodities, and to sell their own cheaper.

As far as it relates to the tendency of a free coinage to produce an increase of expense in different ways that have been stated, the argument must be allowed to have foundation both in reason and in experience. It describes what has been exemplified in Great Britain.

The effect of giving an artificial value to bullion, is not at first sight obvious; but it actually happened at the period immediately preceding the late reformation in the gold coin of the country just named. A pound troy of gold bullion, of standard fineness, was then from 19*s*. 6*d*. to 25*s*. sterling dearer than an equal weight of guineas, as delivered at the mint. The phenomen is thus accounted for—the old guineas were more than two per cent. lighter than their *standard weight*. This *weight*, therefore, in bullion, was truly worth two per cent. more than those guineas. It consequently had, in respect to them, a correspondent rise in the market.

And as guineas were then current by *tale*, the new ones, as they issued from the mint, were confounded in circulation with the old ones; and, by association, were depreciated below their intrinsic value, in comparison with bullion. It became, of course, a profitable traffic, to sell bullion for coin, to select the light pieces and re-issue them in currency, and to melt down the heavy ones, and sell them again as bullion. This practice, besides other inconveniences, cost the Government large sums in the renewal of the coins.

But the remainder of the argument stands upon ground far more questionable. It depends upon very numerous and very complex combinations, in which there is infinite latitude for fallacy and error.

The most plausible part of it is that which relates to the course of exchange. Experience in France has shown that the market price of bullion has been influenced by the mint difference between that and coin—sometimes to the full extent of the difference; and it would seem to be a clear inference, that whenever that difference materially exceeded the charges of remitting bullion from the country where it existed, to another in which coinage is free, exchange would be in favor of the former.

If, for instance, the balance of trade between France and England were at any time equal, their merchants would naturally have reciprocal payments to make to an equal amount, which, as usual, would be liquidated by means of bills of exchange. If, in this situation, the difference between coin and bullion should be in the market, as at the mint of France, eight per cent.; if, also, the charges of transporting money from France to England should not be above two per cent.; and if exchange should be at par, it is evident that a profit of six per cent. might be made, by sending bullion from France to England, and drawing bills for the amount. One hundred louis d'ors in coin, would purchase the weight of one hundred and eight in bullion; one hundred of which, remitted to England, would suffice to pay a debt of an equal amount; and two being paid for the charges of insurance and transportation, there would remain six for the benefit of the person who should manage the negotiation. But as so large a profit could not fail to produce competition, the bills, in consequence of this, would decrease in price, till the profit was reduced to the *minimum* of an adequate recompense for the trouble and risk. And, as the amount of one hundred louis d'ors in England, might be afforded for ninety-six in France, with a profit of more than one and a half per cent., bills upon England might fall in France to four per cent. below par; one per cent. being a sufficient profit to the exchanger or broker for the management of the business.

But it is *admitted* that this advantage is lost, when the balance of trade is against the nation which imposes the duty in question; because, by increasing the demand for bullion, it brings this to a par with the coins; and it is to be *suspected*, that where commercial principles have their free scope, and are well understood, the market difference between the metals in coin and bullion, will seldom approximate to that of the mint, if the latter be considerable. It must be not a little difficult to keep the money of the world, which can be employed to an equal purpose in the commerce of the world, in a state of degradation, in comparison with the money of a particular country.

This alone would seem sufficient to prevent it; whenever the price of coin to bullion, in the market, materially exceeded the par of the metals, it would become an object to send the bullion abroad, if not to pay a foreign balance, to be invested in some other way in foreign countries, where it bore a superior value; an operation by which immense fortunes might be amassed, if it were not that the exportation of the bullion would of itself restore the intrinsic par. But, as it would naturally have this effect, the advantage supposed would contain in itself the principle of its own destruction. As long, however, as the exportation of bullion could be made with profit, which is as long as exchange could remain below par, there would be a drain of the gold and silver of the country.

If anything can maintain, for a length of time, a material difference between the value of the metals in coin and in bullion, it must be a constant and considerable balance of trade in favor of the country in which it is maintained. In one situated like the United States, it would in all probability be a hopeless attempt. The frequent demand for gold and silver, to pay balances to foreigners, would tend powerfully to preserve the equilibrium of intrinsic value.

The prospect is, that it would occasion foreign coins to circulate by common consent, nearly at par with the national.

MONETARY LEGISLATION. 57

To say, that as far as the effect of lowering exchange is produced, though it be only occasional and momentary, there is a benefit the more thrown in the scale of public prosperity, is not satisfactory. It has been seen, that it may be productive of one evil, the investment of a part of the national capital in foreign countries; which can hardly be beneficial but in a situation like that of the United Netherlands, where an immense capital, and a decrease of internal demand, render it necessary to find employment for money in the wants of other nations; and, perhaps on a close examination, other evils may be descried.

One allied to that which has been mentioned is this—taking France, for the sake of more concise illustration, as the scene. Whenever it happens that French louis d'ors are sent abroad, from whatever cause, if there be a considerable difference between coin and bullion in the market of France, it will constitute an advantageous traffic to send back these louis d'ors, and bring away bullion in lieu of them; upon all which exchanges, France must sustain an actual loss of a part of its gold and silver.

Again: such a difference between coin and bullion may tend to counteract a favorable balance of trade. Whenever the foreign merchant is the carrier of his own commodities to France for sale, he has a strong inducement to bring back specie, instead of French commodities; because a return in the latter may afford no profit, may even be attended with loss; in the former, it will afford a certain profit. The same principle must be supposed to operate in the general course of remittances from France to other countries. The principal question with a merchant naturally is, in what manner can I realize a given sum, with most advantage, where I wish to place it? And, in cases in which other commodities are not likely to produce equal profit with bullion, it may be expected that this will be preferred; to which, the greater certainty attending the operation must be an additional incitement. There can hardly be imagined a circumstance less friendly to trade, than the existence of an extra inducement arising from the possibility of a profitable speculation upon the articles themselves, to export from a country its gold and silver, rather than the products of its land and labor.

The other advantages supposed, of obliging foreigners to pay dearer for domestic commodities, and to sell their own cheaper, are applied to a situation which includes a favorable balance of trade. It is understood in this sense: the prices of domestic commodities (such, at least, as are peculiar to to the country) remain attached to the denominations of the coins. When a favorable balance of trade realizes in the market the mint difference between coin and bullion, foreigners who must pay in the latter, are obliged to give more of it for such commodities than they otherwise would do. Again: the bullion, which is now obtained at a cheaper rate in the home market, will procure the same quantity of goods in the foreign market as before, which is said to render foreign commodities cheaper. In this reasoning, much fallacy is to be suspected. If it be true that foreigners pay more for domestic commodities, it must be equally true that they get more for their own when they bring them themselves to market. If peculiar or other domestic commodities adhere to the denominations of the coins, no reason occurs why foreign commidities of a like character should not do the same thing; and in this case, the foreigner, though he receive only the same value in coin for his merchandise as formerly, can convert it into a greater quantity of bullion. Whence the nation is liable to lose more of its gold and silver than if their intrinsic value in relation to the coins were preserved. And whether the gain or the loss will, on the whole, preponderate, would appear to depend on the comparative proportion of active commerce of the one country with the other.

It is evident, also, that the nation must pay as much gold and silver as before, for the commodities which it procures *abroad;* and whether it obtains this gold and silver cheaper, or not, turns upon the solution of the question just intimated, respecting the relative proportion of active commerce between the two countries.

Besides these considerations, it is admitted in the reasoning, that the advantages supposed, which depend on a favorable balance of trade, have a tendency to affect that balance disadvantageously. Foreigners, it is allowed, will in this case seek some other vent for their commodities, and some other market where they can supply their wants at an easier rate. A tendency of this kind, if real, would be a sufficient objection to the regulation. Nothing which contributes to change a beneficial current of trade, can well compensate, by particular advantages, for so injurious an effect. It is far more easy to transfer trade from a less to a more favorable channel, than, when once transferred, to bring it back to its old one. Every source of artificial interruption to an advantageous current, is, therefore, cautiously to be avoided.

It merits attention, that the able minister, who lately and so long presided over the finances of France, does not attribute to the duty of coinage in that country, any particular advantages in relation to exchange and trade. Though he rather appears an advocate for it, it is on the sole ground of the revenue it affords, which he represents as in the nature of a very moderate duty on the general mass of exportation.

And it is not improbable that, to the singular felicity of situation of that kingdom, is to be attributed its not having been sensible of the evils which seem incident to the regulation. There is, perhaps, no part of Europe which has so little need of other countries as France. Comprehending a variety of soils and climates, an immense population, its agriculture in a state of mature improvement, it possesses within its own bosom, most, if not all, the productions of the earth, which any of its most favored neighbors can boast. The variety, abundance, and excellence of its wines, constitute a peculiar advantage in its favor. Arts and manufactures are there also in a very advanced state; some of them, of considerable importance, in higher perfection than elsewhere. Its contiguity to Spain; the intimate nature of its connection with that country; a country with few fabrics of its own, consequently numerous wants, and the principal receptacle of the treasures of the New World: These circumstances concur, in securing to France so uniform and so considerable a balance of trade, as in a great measure to counteract the natural tendency of any errors which may exist in the system of her mint; and to render inferences from the operation of that system there, in reference to this country, more liable to mislead than to instruct. Nor ought it to pass unnoticed, that, with all these advantages, the government of France has found it necessary, on some occasions, to employ very violent methods to compel the bringing of bullion to the mint; a circumstance which affords a strong presumption of the inexpediency of the regulation, and of the impracticability of executing it in the United States.

This point has been the longer dwelt upon, not only because there is a diversity of opinion among speculative men concerning it, and a diversity in the practice of the most considerable commercial nations, but because the acts of our own government, under the confederation, have not only admitted the expediency of defraying the expense of coinage out of the metals themselves, but upon this idea have both made a deduction from the weight of the coins, and established a difference between their regulated price and the mint price of bullion, greater than would result from that deduction. This double operation in favor of a principle so questionable in itself, has made a more particular investigation of it a duty.

The intention, however, of the preceding remarks, is rather to show that the expectation of commercial advantages ought not to decide in favor of a duty on coinage, and that, if it should be adopted, it ought not to be in the form of a deduction from the intrinsic value of the coins, than absolutely to exclude the idea of any difference whatever between the value of the metals in coin and in bullion. It is not clearly discerned that a small difference between the mint price of bullion, and the regulated value of the coins, would be pernicious, or that it might not even be advisable, in the first instance, by way of experiment, merely as a preventive to the melting down and exportation of the coins. This will now be somewhat more particularly considered.

The arguments for a coinage entirely free, are, that it preserves the intrinsic value of the metals; that it makes the expense of fabrication a general instead of a partial tax; and that it tends to promote the abundance of gold and silver, which, it is alleged, will flow to that place where they find the best price, and from that place where they are in any degree undervalued.

The first consideration has not much weight, as an objection to a plan which, without diminishing the quantity of metals in the coins, merely allows a less price for them in bullion at the national factory or mint. No rule of intrinsic value is violated, by considering the raw material as worth less than the fabric, in proportion to the expense of fabrication. And by divesting foreign coins of the privilege of circulating as money, they become the raw material.

The second consideration has perhaps greater weight. But it may not amount to an objection, if it be the best method of preventing disorders in the coins, which it is in a particular manner the interest of those on whom the tax would fall to prevent. The practice of taking gold by weight, which has of late years obtained in Great Britain, has been found, in some degree, a remedy: but this is inconvenient, and may on that account fall into into disuse. Another circumstance has had a remedial operation. This is the delays of the mint. It appears to be the practice there, not to make payment for the bullion which is brought to be exchanged for coin, till it either has in fact, or is pretended to have, undergone the process of recoining.

The necessity of fulfilling prior engagements is a cause or pretext for postponing the delivery of the coin in lieu of the bullion. And this delay creates a difference in the market price of the two things. Accordingly, for some years past, an ounce of standard gold, which is worth in coin £3 17s. 10½d. sterling, has been in the market of London, in bullion, only £3 17s. 6d., which is within a small fraction of one-half per cent. less. Whether this be management in the mint, to accommodate the bank in the purchase of bullion, or to effect indirectly something equivalent to a formal difference of price, or whether it be the natural course of the business, is open to conjecture.

It at the same time indicates that if the mint were to make prompt payment, at about half per cent. less than it does at present, the state of bullion in respect to coin would be precisely the same as it now is. And it would be then certain that the Government would save expense in the coinage of gold; since it is not probable that the time actually lost in the course of the year, in converting bullion into coin, can be an equivalent to half per cent. on the advance, and there will generally be at the command of the Treasury a considerable sum of money waiting for some periodical disbursement, which, without hazard, might be applied to that advance.

In what sense a free coinage can be said to promote the abundance of gold and silver, may be inferred from the instances which have been given of the tendency of a contrary system to promote their exportation. It is, however, not probable that a very small difference of value between coin and bullion can have any effect which ought to enter into calculation. There can be no inducement of positive profit, to export the bullion, as long as the difference of price is exceeded by the expense of transportation. And the prospect of smaller loss upon the metals than upon commodities, when the difference is very minute, will be frequently overbalanced by the possibility of doing better with the latter, from a rise of markets. It is, at any rate, certain that it can be of no consequence in this view,. whether the superiority of coin to bullion in the market, be produced, as in England, by the delay of the mint, or by a formal discrimination in the regulated values.

Under an impression that a *small* difference between the value of the coin and the mint price of bullion, is the least-exceptionable expedient for restraining the melting down, or exportation of the former, and not perceiving that, if it be a very moderate one, it can be hurtful in other respects—the Secretary is inclined to an experiment of one-half per cent. on each of the metals. The fact which has been mentioned, with regard to the price of gold bullion in the English market, seems to demonstrate that such a difference may safely be made. In this case, there must be immediate payment for the gold and silver offered to the mint. How far one half per cent. will go towards defraying the expense of coinage, cannot be determined beforehand with accuracy. It is presumed that, on an economical plan, it will suffice in relation to gold. But it is not expected that the same rate on silver will be sufficient to defray the expense attending that metal. Some additional provision may therefore be found necessary, if this limit be adopted.

It does not seem to be advisable to make any greater difference in regard to silver than to gold; because it is desirable that the proportion between the two metals in the market should correspond with that in the coins, which would not be the case if the mint price of one was comparatively lower than that of the other; and because, also, silver being proposed to be rated in respect to gold, somewhat below its general commercial value, if there should be a disparity to its disadvantage in the mint prices of the two metals, it would obstruct too much the bringing of it to be coined, and would add an inducement to export it. Nor does it appear to the Secretary safe to make a greater difference between the value of coin and bullion, than has been mentioned. It will be better to have to increase it hereafter, if this shall be found expedient, than to have to recede from too considerable a difference, in consequence of evils which shall have been experienced.

It is sometimes mentioned, as an expedient which, consistently with a free coinage, may serve to prevent the evils desired to be avoided, to incorporate in the coins a greater proportion of alloy than is usual; regulating their value, nevertheless, according to the quantity of pure metal they contain. This, it is supposed, by adding to the difficulty of refining them, would cause bullion to be preferred both for manufacture and exportation.

But strong objections lie against this scheme:—an augmentation of expense; an actual depreciation of the coin; a danger of still greater depreciation in the public opinion; the facilitating of counterfeits; while it is questionable whether it would have the effect expected from it.

The alloy being esteemed of no value, an increase of it is evidently an increase of expense. This, in relation to the gold coins, particularly, is a matter of moment. It has been noted, that the alloy in them consists partly of silver. If, to avoid expense, the addition should be of copper only, this would spoil the appearance of the coin, and give it a base countenance. Its beauty would, indeed, be injured, though in a less degree, even if the usual proportions of silver and copper should be maintained in the increased quantity of alloy.

And however inconsiderable an additional expenditure of copper in the coinage of a year may be deemed, in a series of years it would become of consequence. In regulations which contemplate the lapse and operation of ages, a very small item of expense acquires importance.

The actual depreciation of the coin by an increase of alloy, results from the very circumstance which is the motive to it—the greater difficulty of refining. In England it is customary for those concerned in manufactures of gold, to make a deduction in the price of four pence sterling per ounce, of fine gold, for every carat which the mass containing it is below the legal standard. Taking this as a rule, an inferiority of a single carat, or one twenty-fourth part in the gold coins of the United States, compared with the English standard, would cause the *same quantity* of pure gold in them to be worth nearly four-tenths per cent. less than in the coins of Great Britain. This circumstance would be likely, in process of time, to be felt in the market of the United States.

A still greater depreciation, in the public opinion, would be to be apprehended from the *apparent* debasement of the coin. The effects of imagination and prejudice cannot be safely disregarded in anything that relates to money. If the beauty of the coin be impaired, it may be found difficult to satisfy the generality of the community that what appears worse is not really less valuable; and it is not altogether certain that an impression of its being so may not occasion an unnatural argumentation of prices.

Greater danger of imposition, by counterfeits, is also to be apprehended from the injury which will be done to the appearance of the coin. It is a just observation, that "the perfcetion of the coins is a great safeguard against counterfeits." And it is evident that the color, as well as the excellence of the workmanship, is an ingredient in that perfection. The intermixture of too much alloy, particularly of copper, in the gold coins at least, must materially lessen the facility of distinguishing, by the eye, the purer from the baser kind, the genuine from the counterfeit.

The inefficiency of the arrangement to the purpose intended to be answered by it, is rendered probable by different considerations. If the standard of plate in the United States should be regulated according to that of the national coins, it is to be expected that the goldsmith would prefer these to the foreign coins, because he would find them prepared to his hand, in the state which he desires; whereas he would have to *expend* an additional quantity of alloy to bring the foreign coins to that state. If the standard of plate, by law or usage, should be superior to that of the national coins, there would be a possibility of the foreign coins bearing a higher price in the market; and this would not only obstruct their being brought to the mint, but might occasion the exportation of the national coin in preference. It is not understood that the practice of making an abatement of price for the inferiority of standard is applicable to the English mint; and if it be not, this would also contribute to frustrating the expected effect from the increase of alloy. For, in this case, a given quantity of pure metal, in our standard, would be worth as much there as in bullion of the English or any other standard.

Considering therefore, the uncertainty of the success of the expedient, and the inconveniences which seem incident to it, it would appear preferable to submit to those of a free coinage. It is observable, that additional expense, which is one of the principal of these, is also applicable to the proposed remedy.

It is now proper to resume and finish the answer to the first question, in order to which the three succeeding ones have necessarily been anticipated. The conclusion to be drawn from the observations which have been made on the subject is this: That the unit, in the coins of the United States, ought to correspond with 24 grains and ¾ of a grain of pure gold, and with 371 grains and ¼ of a grain of pure silver, each answering to a dollar in the money of account. The former is exactly agreeable to the present value of gold, and the latter is within a small fraction of the mean of the two last emissions of dollars—the only ones which are now found in common circulation, and of which the newest is in the greatest abundance. The alloy in each case to be one-twelfth of the total weight, which will make the unit 27 grains of standard gold, and 405 grains of standard silver.

Each of these, it has been remarked, will answer to a dollar in the money of account. It is conceived that nothing better can be done in relation to this, than to pursue the track marked out by the resolution of the 8th of August, 1786. This has been approved abroad, as well as at home, and it is certain that nothing can be more simple and convenient than the decimal subdivisions. There is every reason to expect that the method will speedily grow into general use, when it shall be seconded by corresponding coins. On this plan, the unit in the money of account will continue to be, as established by that resolution, a dollar; and its multiples, dimes, cents, and mills, or tenths, hundredths, and thousandths.

MONETARY LEGISLATION. 63

NUMBER, DENOMINATIONS, ETC., OF THE COINS.

With regard to the number of different pieces which shall compose the coins of the United States, two things are to be consulted—convenience of circulation, and cheapness of the coinage. The first ought not to be sacrificed to the last; but as far as they can be reconciled to each other, it is desirable to do it. Numerous and small (if not too minute) subdivisions assist circulation; but the multiplication of the smaller kinds increases expense; the same process being necessary to a small as to a large piece.

As is is easy to add, it will be most adviseable to begin with a small number, till experience shall decide whether any other kinds are necessary. The following, it is conceived, will be sufficient in the commencement:

One gold piece, equal in weight and value to ten units or dollars.

One gold piece, equal to a tenth part of the former, and which shall be a unit or dollar.

One silver piece, which shall also be a unit or dollar.

One silver piece, which shall be, in weight and value, a tenth part of the silver unit or dollar.

One copper piece, which shall be of the value of a hundredth part of a dollar.

One other copper piece, which shall be half the value of the former.

It is not proposed that the lightest of the two gold coins should be numerous, as, in large payments, the larger the pieces the shorter the process of counting, the less risk of mistake, and, consequently, the greater the safety and the convenience; and, in small payments, it is not perceived that any inconvenience can accrue from an entire dependence on the silver and copper coins. The chief inducement to the establishment of the small gold piece, is to have a sensible object in that metal, as well as in silver, to express the unit. Fifty thousand at a time in circulation, may suffice for this purpose.

The tenth part of a dollar is but a small piece, and, with the aid of the copper coins, will probably suffice for all the more minute uses of circulation. It is less than the least of the silver coins now in general currency in England.

The largest copper piece will nearly answer to the half-penny sterling, and the smallest, of course, to the farthing. Pieces of very small value are a great accommodation, and the means of a beneficial economy to the poor, by enabling them to purchase, in small portions, and at a more reasonable rate, the necessaries of which they stand in need. If there are only cents, the lowest price for any portion of a vendable commodity, however inconsiderable in quantity, will be a cent; if there are half cents, it will be a half-cent; and, in a great number of cases, exactly the same things will be sold for a half-cent, which, if there were none, would cost a cent. But a half-cent is low enough for the *minimum* of price. Excessive minuteness would defeat its object. To enable the poorer classes to procure necessaries cheap, is to enable them, with more comfort to themselves, to labor for less; the advantages of which need no comment.

The denominations of the silver coins contained in the resolution of the 8th of August, 1796, are conceived to be significant and proper. The dollar is recommended by its correspondency with the present coin of that name for which it is designed to be a substitute, which will facilitate its ready adoption as such in the minds of the citizens. The dime, or tenth, the cent, or hundredth, the mill, or thousandth, are proper, because they express the proportions which they are intended to designate. It is only to be regretted that the meaning of these terms will not be familiar to those who are not acquainted with the language from which they are borrowed. It were to be wished that the length, and, in some degree, the clumsiness of some of the corresponding terms in English did not discourage from preferring them. It is useful to have names which signify the two things to which they belong; and, in respect to objects of general use, in a manner intelligible to all. Perhaps it might be an improvement to let the dollar have the appellation either of dollar or unit, (which last will be the more significant,) and to substitute "tenth" for dime. In time, the unit may succeed to the dollar. The word "cent," being in use in various transactions and instruments, will, without much difficulty, be understood as the hundredth; and the half-cent, of course, as the two hundredth part.

The eagle is not a very expressive or apt appellation for the larger gold piece; but nothing better occurs. The smallest of the two gold coins many be called the dollar or unit, in common with the silver piece, with which it coincides.

The volume or size of each piece is a matter of more consequence than its denomination. It is evident that the more superficies or surface, the more the piece will be liable to be injured by frictton; or, in other words, the faster it will wear. For this reason, it is desirable to render the thickness as great, in proportion to the breadth, as may consist with neatness and good appearance. Hence, the form of the double guinea, or double louis-d'or, is preferable to that of the half johannes for the large gold piece. The small one cannot well be of any other size than the Portuguese piece of eight of the same metal.

As it is of consequence to fortify the idea of the identity of the dollar, it may be best to let the form and size of the new one, as far as the quantity of matter (the alloy being less) permits, agree with the form and size of the present. The diameter may be the same.

The tenth may be in a mean between the Spauish $\frac{1}{8}$ and $\frac{1}{16}$ of a dollar.

The copper coins may be formed merely with a view to good appearance, as any difference in the wearing that can result from difference of form, can be of little consequence in reference to that metal.

It is conceived that the weight of the cent may be eleven pennyweights; which will about correspond with the value of the copper and the expense of coinage. This will be to conform to the rule of intrinsic value, as far as regard to the convenient size of the coins will permit: and the deduction of the expense of coinage in this case will be the more proper, as the copper coins, which have been current hitherto, have passed till lately for much more than their intrinsic value. Taking the weight as has been suggested, the size of the cent may be nearly that of the piece herewith transmitted, which weighs 1odwt. 11grs. 10m. Two-thirds of the diameter of the cent will suffice for the diameter of the half cent.

It may, perhaps, be thought expedient, according to general practice, to make the copper coinage an object of profit; but where this is done to any considerable extent, it is hardly possible to have effectual security against counterfeits. This consideration, concurring with the soundness of the principle of preserving the intrinsic value of the money of a country, seems to outweigh the consideration of profit.

The foregoing suggestions, respecting the sizes of the several coins, are made on the supposition that the legislature may think fit to regulate this matter. Perhaps, however, it may be judged not unadvisable to leave it to executive discretion.

With regard to the proposed size of the cent, it is to be confessed, that it is rather greater than might be wished, if it could with propriety and safety be made less; and should the value of copper continue to decline, as it has done for some time past, it is very questionable whether it will long remain alone a fit metal for money. This has led to a consideration of the expediency of uniting a small proportion of silver with the copper, in order to be able to lessen the bulk of the inferior coins. For this, there are precedents in several parts of Europe. In France, the composition which is called billion has consisted of one part silver and four parts copper; according to which proportion, a cent might contain seventeen grains, defraying out of the material, the expense of coinage. The conveniency of size is a recommendation of such a species of coin; but the Secretary is deterred from proposing it, by the apprehension of counterfeits. The effect of so small a quantity of silver, in comparatively so large a quantity of copper, could easily be imitated, by a mixture of other metals of little value, and the temptation to doing it would not be inconsiderable.

The devices of the coins are far from being matters of indifference, as they may be made the vehicles of useful impressions. They ought, therefore, to be emblematical, but without losing sight of simplicity. The fewer sharp points and angles there are, the less will be the loss by wearing. The Secretary thinks it best, on this head, to confine himself to these concise and general remarks.

The last point to be discussed, respects the currency of foreign coins.

The abolition of this, in proper season, is a necessary part of the system contemplated for the national coinage. But this it will be expedient to defer, till some considerable progress has been made in preparing substitutes for them. A gradation may therefore be found most convenient.

The foreign coins may be suffered to circulate, precisely upon their present footing, for one year after the mint shall have commenced its operations. The privilege may then be continued for another year, to the gold coins of Portugal, England, and France, and to the silver coins of Spain. And these may still be permitted to be current for one year more, at the rates allowed to be given for them at the mint; after the expiration of which the circulation of all foreign coins to cease.

The moneys which will be paid into the Treasury during the first year, being recoined before they are issued anew, will afford a partial substitute, before any interruption is given to the pre-existing supplies of circulation. The revenues of the succeeding year, and the coins which will be brought to the mint, in consequence of the discontinuance of their currency, will materially extend the substitute in course of that year; and its extension will be so far increased, during the third year, by the facility of securing the remaining species to be recoined, which will arise from the diminution of their current values, as probably to enable the dispensing wholly with the circulation of the foreign coins after that period. The progress which the currency of bank bills will be likely to have made, during the same time, will also afford a substitute of another kind.

This arrangement, besides avoiding a sudden stagnation of circulation, will cause a considerable proportion of whatever loss may be incident to to the establishment, in the first instance, to fall, as it ought to do, upon the Government, and will probably tend to distribute the remainder of it more equally among the community.

It may, nevertheless, be advisable, in addition to the precautions here suggested, to repose a discretionary authority in the President of the United States, to continue the currency of the Spanish dollar, at a value corresponding with the quantity of fine silver contained in it, beyond the period above mentioned, for the cessation of the circulation of the foreign coins. It is possible that an exception in favor of this particular species of coin may be found expedient; and it may tend to obviate inconveniences, if there be a power to make the exception, in a capacity to be exerted when the period shall arrive.

The Secretary for the Department of the State, in his report to the House of Representatives, on the subject of establishing a uniformity in the weights, measures, and coins of the United States, has proposed that the weight of the dollar should correspond with the unit of weight. This was done on the supposition that it would require but a very small addition to the quantity of metal which the dollar, independently on the object he had in view, ought to contain; in which he was guided by the resolution of the 8th of August, 1786, fixing the dollar at 375 grains and 64 hundredths of a grain.

Taking this as the proper standard of the dollar, a small alteration, for the sake of incorporating so systematic an idea, would appear desirable. But, if the principles which have been reasoned from, in this report, are just, the execution of of that idea becomes more difficult. It would certainly not be advisable to make on that account, so considerable a change in the money unit, as would be produced by the addition of five grains of silver to the proper weight of the dollar, without a proportional augmentation, of its relative value; and to make such an augmentation, would be to abandon the advantage of preserving the identity of the dollar, or to speak more accurately, of having the proposed one received and considered as a mere substitute for the present.

The end may, however, be obtained, without either of these inconveniences, by increasing the proportion of alloy in the silver coins. But this would destroy the uniformity, in that respect, between the gold and silver coins. It remains, therefore, to elect which of the two systematic ideas shall be pursued or relinquished; and it may be remarked, that it will be more easy to convert the present silver coins into the proposed ones, if these last have the same, or nearly the same proportion of alloy, than if they have less.

The organization of the Mint, yet remains to be considered.

This relates to the persons to be employed, and to the services which they are respectively to perform. It is conceived that there ought to be—

A Director of the Mint; to have the general superintendence of the business.

An Assay Master, or Assayer; to receive the metals brought to the Mint, ascertain their fineness, and deliver them to be coined.

A Master Coiner; to conduct the making of the coins.

A Cashier; to receive and pay them out.

An Auditor; to keep and adjust the accounts of the Mint.

Clerks; as many as the Directors of the Mint shall deem necessary, to assist the different officers.

Workmen; as many as may be found requisite.

A Porter.

In several of the European Mints, there are various other officers, but the foregoing are those who only appear to be indispensable.

Persons in the capacity of clerks will suffice instead of the others, with the advantage of greater economy.

The number of workmen is left indefinite, because, at certain times, it is requisite to have more than at others. They will, however, never be numerous. The expense of the establishment, in an ordinary year, will probably be from fifteen to twenty thousand dollars.

The remedy for errors in the weight and alloy of the coins, must necessarily form a part, in the system of a mint; and the manner of applying it will require to be regulated. The following account is given of the practice in England, in this particular:

A certain number of pieces are taken promiscuously out of every fifteen pounds of gold, coined at the Mint, which are deposited, for safe keeping, in a strong box, called the pix. This box, from time to time, is opened in the presence of the Lord Chancellor, the officers of the Treasury, and others, and portions are selected from the pieces of each coinage, which are melted together, and the mass assayed by a jury of the Company of Goldsmiths. If the imperfection and deficiency, both in fineness and weight, fall short of a sixth of a carat, or 40 grains of pure gold, upon a pound of standard, the master of the Mint is held excusable; because it is supposed, that no workman can reasonably be answerable for greater exactness. The expediency of some similar regulation seems to be manifest.

All which is humbly submitted,

ALEXANDER HAMILTON,
Secretary of the Treasury.

The establishment of the double standard in the United States was due to Alexander Hamilton; and the act of April 2, 1792 (1 Stat. L., p. 246), is the first law that established that standard in any country. Indeed, the double standard, properly so called, was something unknown in monetary legislation until introduced in the United States by the act above named. The principal provisions of that act are as follows:

[April 2, 1792.)

SEC. 9. *And be it further enacted*, That there shall be from time to time struck and coined at the said mint, coins of gold, silver, and copper, of the following denominations, viz.: *Eagles*, each to be of the value of ten dollars or units, and to contain two-hundred and forty-seven grains and four-eighths of a grain of pure or two hundred and seventy grains of standard gold. *Half eagles*, each to be of the value of five dollars, and to contain one hundred and twenty-three grains and six-eighths of a grain of pure, or one hundred and thirty-five grains of standard gold. *Quarter eagles*, each to be of the value of two dollars and a half dollar, and to contain sixty-one grains and seven-eighths of a grain of pure, or sixty-seven grains and four-eights of a grain of standard gold. *Dollars or units*, each to be of the value of a Spanish milled dollar as the same is now current, and to contain three hundred and seventy-one grains and four-sixteenths parts of a grain of pure, or four hundred and sixteen grains of standard silver. *Half dollars*, each to be of half the value of the dollar or unit, and to contain one hundred and eighty-five grains and ten-sixteenth parts of a grain of pure, or two hundred and eight grains of standard silver. *Quarter dollars*, each to be of one-fourth the value of the dollar or unit, and to contain ninety-two grains and thirteen-sixteenth parts of a grain of pure, or one hundred and four grains of standard silver. *Dismes*, each to be of the value of one-tenth of a dollar or unit, and to contain thirty-seven grains and two-sixteenth parts of a grain of pure, or forty-one grains and three-fiith parts of a grain of standard silver. *Half dismes*, each to be of the value of one-twentieth of a dollar, and to contain eighteen grains and nine-sixteenth parts of a grain of pure, or twenty grains and four-fifth parts of a grain of standard silver. *Cents*, each to be of the value of the one-hundredth part of a dollar, and to contain eleven penny-weights of copper. *Half cents*, each to be of the value of half a cent, and to contain five penny-weights and half a penny-weight of copper.

SEC. 11. *And be it further enacted*, That the proportional value of gold to silver in all coins which shall by law be current as money within the United States, shall be as fifteen to one, according to quantity in weight, of pure gold or pure silver; that is to say, every fifteen pounds weight of pure silver shall be of equal value in all payments, with one pound weight of pure gold, and so on in proportion as to any greater or less quantities of the respective metals.

SEC. 12. *And be it further enacted*, That the standard for all gold coins of the United States shall be eleven points fine to one alloy; and accordingly, that eleven parts in twelve of the entire weight of each of the said coins shall consist of pure gold, and the remaining one-twelfth part of alloy; and the said alloy shall be composed of silver and copper, in such proportions not exceeding one-half silver as shall be found convenient; to be regulated by the Director of the Mint, for the time being, with the approbation of the President of the United States, until further provision shall be made by law. And to the end that the necessary information may be had in order to the making of such further provision, it shall be the duty of the Director of the Mint, at the expiration of a year after commencing the operations of the said Mint, to report to Congress the practice thereof during the said year, touching the composition of the alloy of the said gold coins, the reasons for such practice, and the experiments and observations which shall have been made concerning the effects of different proportions of silver and copper in the said alloy.

SEC. 13. *And be it further enacted*, That the standard for all silver coins of the United States, shall be one thousand four hundred and eighty-five parts fine to one hundred and seventy-nine parts alloy, and accordingly that one thousand four hundred and eighty-five parts in one thousand six hundred and sixty-four parts of the entire weight of each of the said coins shall consist of pure silver, and the remaining one hundred and seventy-nine parts of alloy; which alloy shall be wholly of copper.

SEC. 16. *And be it further enacted*, That all the gold and silver coins which shall have been struck at, and issued from the said Mint, shall be a lawful tender in all payments whatsoever, those of full weight according to the respective values hereinbefore declared, and those of less than full weight at values proportional to their respective weights.

SEC. 20. *And be it further enacted*, That the money of account of the United States shall be expressed in dollars or units, dismes or tenths, cents or hundredths, and milles or thousandths, a disme being the tenth part of a dollar, a cent the hundredth part of a dollar, a mille the thousandth part of a dollar, and that all accounts in the public offices and all proceedings in the courts of the United States, shall be kept and had in conformity to this regulation.

Approved, April 2, 1792.

ANALYSIS OF HAMILTON'S REPORT.

An analysis of Hamilton's report on the establishment of a mint shows that, while his convictions inclined him to the gold standard, if only one metal was to constitute our full legal-tender currency, expediency and the necessity of providing the country with a sufficient amount of currency, which he believed could not be furnished at the time by the use of gold alone, induced him to recommend the double standard with a fixed ratio in coinage between the two metals. His reason for preferring gold, if only one metal were employed, was that gold was less liable to variations of value than silver; for Hamilton had a clear conception of the truth that the metal of which the monetary medium consists, in order to constitute a just measure of the value of all other things, should itself be subject to as few and as slight fluctuations of value as is in the nature of things possible, and that a metal subject to great and sudden changes of value was utterly unfit for such a purpose.

"As long," he says, "as gold, either from its intrinsic superiority as a metal, from its rarity, or from the prejudices of mankind, retains so considerable a pre-eminence in value over silver as it has hitherto had, a natural consequence of this seems to be that its condition will be more stationary. The revolutions, therefore, which may take place in the comparative value of gold and silver will be changes in the state of the latter rather than in that of the former."

The language here used leads to the conclusion that the relative increase or decrease of the production of gold or silver was a cause of change in their relative stability of value with which Hamilton did not concern himself. Nor was there any reason why he should, since the relative production of gold and silver in the world from 1780 to 1820 was probably more uniform as to value than it ever was before or ever has been since for an equal period of time, the value of the gold averaging very nearly 24 per cent. and that of the silver 76 per cent. of the total value of the production of the precious metals from 1781 to 1821. Still less had he to take into consideration the production of the money metals in the United States, for the country had in his time produced little or none of them, and there were no indications that it would at any near date produce them in any large quantities.

The causes of change in the comparative value of gold and silver which he had in view were confined to those mentioned in the above and in the following extract:

<blockquote>Gold may, perhaps, in certain senses, be said to have a greater stability than silver, as being of superior value; less liberties have been taken with it in the regulations of different countries. Its standard has remained more uniform, and it has in other respects undergone fewer changes, as, being not so much an article of merchandise, owing to the use made of silver in the trade with the East Indies and China, it is less liable to be influenced by circumstances of commercial demand. And if, reasoning by analogy, it could be affirmed that there is a physical probability of greater proportional increase in the quantity of silver than in that of gold, it would afford an additional reason for calculating on greater steadiness in the value of the latter.</blockquote>

This prediction that the revolutions which might take place in the relative value of the two metals would be changes in the state of silver rather than in that of gold was soon fulfilled.

Hamilton's reasons for the recommendation of the double standard, with a gold unit as well as a silver unit of value, are very plainly stated by him in his report. He did not deem it advisable to attach the unit exclusively to either of the metals—a view in which Jefferson fully agreed with him, writing to Hamilton, who had sent him his report: "I concur with you in thinking that the unit must stand on both metals,"—and hence one of his recommendations was that there should be stamped a gold piece of the denomination of one dollar in order to have "a sensible object in that metal as well as in silver to express the unit."

The coinage of the gold dollar, however, was not provided for by the act of April 2, 1792. The eagle having been made by that act the basis of the gold coins, it became the sensible representative of the gold-money unit, containing, as the law declared it should, ten gold dollars or nnits.

Hamilton did not recommend attaching the unit exclusively to either metal, because that could not be done without destroying the office and character of one of them as money, without abridging the quantity of the circulating medium, and without diminishing the utility of one of the metals. The country at that time was in no condition to bear a lessening of the amount of the circulating medium, for it was still suffering grievously from the widespread commercial ruin produced by the worthless Continental paper, which had driven metallic money out of use.

When Hamilton wrote, the single gold standard had not yet been adopted by monetary legislation in any country. Not until a quarter of a century later was it made the basis of the monetary system of England; and its adoption by the United States in 1792 would have encountered almost insuperable obstacles. An abundant specic currency was needed. The use of silver was rooted in the commercial habits of the people. There was little or no gold in general circulation. Hence, silver had to be retained and gold added to it if a sufficiency of currency for the needs of commerce was to be procured. The object, to which Hamilton was disposed to make all else subservient in his scheme in so far as it could be done without sacrificing correct monetary principles, was the securing of metallic money in abundance. He thought that by attaching the unit to both metals, silver might be retained as the money of the country, and that gold money might be added to it. Hence his recommendation of the double satndard.

This point having been settled, Hamilton approaches the next, that relating to the ratio:

"If then," he says, "the unit ought to be attached exclusively to neither of the metals, the proportion which ought to subsist between them in the coin becomes a preliminary inquiry, in order to a proper adjustment. * * * In establishing a proportion between the metals there seemt to be an opinion of one of two things:

"To approach as nearly as it can be ascertained the mean or average proportion in what may be called the commercial world, or to retain that which now exists in the United States."

Unfortunately, Hamilton thought that to ascertain the first with precision would require better information than was then possessed or then could be procured without inconvenient delay, but fortunately the ratio he finally concluded to recommend was, although he was not aware of it, the exact ratio, within an almost negligible fraction, in the commercial world. In his report he adopted this ratio by adopting the ratio in this country at the time. At present the commercial ratio of value between gold and silver is, owing to the facility of intercourse between nations due to steam and electricity, the same the world over, allowance being made for the cost of transportation, insurance, etc., from one place to another. It was not so completely so in Hamilton's time, nor was the collection of information as to the ratio between the two precious metals in the various countries of the world as easy then as it would be now. It is therefore not a matter of surprise that he chose to retain the ratio which at the time existed in the United States. Yet, in deciding to adopt this latter proportion, he took pains to show that it did not depart very widely from the one that obtained simultaneously in England, Holland and Spain. It is significant that he repudiated the inference which might possibly be implied that he favored the ratio of 1 to 15 because Sir Isaac Newton, in a representation to the treasury of Great Britain in the year 1717, after stating the particular proportions in the different countries of Europe, concluded:

> By the course of trade and exchange between nation and nation in all Europe fine gold is to fine silver as 14⅘ or 15 to 1.

"However accurated and decisive this authority may be deemed," says Hamilton, "in relation to the period to which it applies, it can not be taken at the distance of more than seventy years as a ratio for determining the existing proportion;"—words which they will do well to ponder who think that the ratio in coinage of gold and silver can be determined for a later by an earlier generation. Hamilton's view was that the ratio in coinage of the two metals should be their commercial ratio; in other words, that the value of the fine metal in a coin, whether gold or silver, should be, so far as practicable, the saue as its value in the form of bullion. "There can," he says, "hardly be a better rule in any country for the legal than the market proportion, if this can be supposed to have been produced by the free and steady course of commercial principles. The presumption in such case is that each metal finds its true level, according to its intrinsic utility, in the general system of money operations." In this he was in entire accord with Jefferson, who wrote:

> Just principles will lead us to inquire into the market price of gold in the several countries with which we shall be principally connected in commerce, and to take an average from them.

In carrying out the plan suggested by Hamilton, Congress,

in the act of April 2, 1792, departed only slightly from his recommendations.

The standard weight of the dollar was fixed at 416 grains, and, as it was to contain 371¼ grains of fine silver, the alloy was about one-ninth. As already noted above, the coinage of the gold one-dollar piece was not authorized, the gold-money unit finding its sensible representative in the eagle, which contained ten.

Divisional silver coins of a weight and fineness corresponding to that of the dollar piece were provided for; that is, 2 half dollars, or 4 quarter dollars, or 10 dimes, contained 371¼ grains of pure silver, the same as the silver dollar. Any cause, therefore, that influenced the circulation of the silver dollar necessarily influenced that of the fractional pieces. Since "free coinage," in the sense above explained, was provided for by the act, there was no "seigniorage" or charge exacted from depositors of bullion at the mint for manufacture into coins. All gold coins and all silver coins, even divisional ones, were made legal tender to an unlimited extent.

There has never been a more perfect example of the double-standard system than that recommended by Hamilton in his report on the establishment of a mint, and embodied in the law of April 2, 1792. Its author has been criticised for not having made every endeavor possible to ascertain the commercial ratio of gold to silver in foreign countries at the time he wrote. From the view-point of abstract monetary principles this criticism is warranted; for no bimetallic system can long continue to exist in a country having an extensive foreign commerce where the ratio of the precious metals in coinage does not agree with their market ratio in foreign lands, particularly in those with which it trades. Had Hamilton, however, made the endeavor to ascertain the market proportional value of gold and silver in foreign lands, and had he been successful in his effort to discover it, he would not, as was remarked above, have been led to a con-

·clusion different from that which he reached by adopting solely the market ratio of the precious metals in the United States.

Thus, though wrong in principle, if even that can be said, since he was contending with a practical difficulty, while he recognized the principle which he did not follow and tells why he did not follow it, he was right in fact, and the bimetallic system of which he was the author did not suffer in the beginning from the adoption of a wrong ratio between the metals.

It soon, however, began to totter under the defect inherent in every bimetallic system, viz.: the impossibility of keeping the mint ratio of the two metals in permanent agreement with their market ratio, a defect which in a bimetallic system calls for repeated remedies, consisting in the changes of the legal ratio to correspond with the ever-shifting market ratio, under penalty of the disappearance from the country of the coins manufactured from the metal undervalued in the mint ratio. This defect was enhanced by a second one in the system recommended by Hamilton by the fact that in it the divisional silver coins were full legal tender and of the same weight and fineness proportionately as the full legal tender silver dollars, two 50-cent pieces, four quarters, or ten dimes containing exactly the same amount of fine silver as the dollar pieces, the consequence of which was, that when silver came to be undervalued in the mint ratio not only the silver dollars were exported, but almost the entire fractional currency, leaving the country with scarcely any small change for ordinary retail transactions. When, as a result of the undervaluation of silver in the ratio, the silver dollar-pieces were exported, the gold full legal tender coins still remained; but when the fractional silver pieces were exported from the same cause, there remained no divisional coins save copper pieces.

Our monetary legislation subsequent to 1792 was intended mainly to correct these two defects. They were the moving causes of the passage of the acts of 1834, 1837, 1853, and 1873.

As the monetary system recommended by Hamilton in his report on the establishment of a mint and enacted into a law on April 2, 1792, was the first instance in history of the bimetallic system proper, so, too, it was the first to illustrate the operations of that system and to demonstrate that what is called the double-standard system of gold and silver, however well poised and adjusted it may be in the beginning, necessarily in time evolves into a single-standard system of either gold or silver—of gold, if silver be undervalued in the ratio, and of silver if gold be the undervalued metal—one of these standards ever alternating with the other, in obedience to Gresham's law, that "if debased coin is attempted to be circulated with full-valued coin, all of the latter will disappear from circulation and the overvalued and debased coin will alone remain, to the ruin of commerce and business."

The United States monetary system established in 1792 is, indeed, as striking a demonstration as can be found in the entire history of monetary arrangements, of the impossibility of maintaining a fixed legal ratio between silver coin and gold coin; and here it may be well to note that this fixed legal ratio of silver to gold has always been the chief impediment in the way of the various attempts at international bimetallism made during the last thirty years, and will probabiy continue to prevent it in the future.

<small>Who would not revolt at the idea of decreeing the obligatory equivalence of two constant quantities of wheat and oats, of cotton and wool, or iron and lead? Under such conditions no honest transaction would be possible, each of these several products being affected, respectively, by dissimilar and variable rises and falls. The force of solidarity of the products would cause inevitable injustice in exchanges. Why should an obligatory equivalence between two determinate weights of gold and silver be more practicable or more legitimate? *</small>

It was remarked above that the law of April 2, 1792, was the first to introduce the double standard, properly so called, into the monetary legislation of any country. It is not intended thereby to convey the erroneous impression that

---

<small>* The Duke de Noailles on the Future of Bimetallism.</small>

gold and silver were not simultaneously coined and put in circulation as monetary instruments previous to the passage of that act. Even before the invention of coinage, gold and silver in bars and rings of a determinate weight were employed as media of payment. The ancients, from the very beginning, considered gold and silver equally entitled to a place in their coinage system.

This simultaneous employment of gold and silver as money has been maintained up to the present time, and has not been discontinued even in countries with the single gold standard. But this simultaneous employment of gold and silver in a country's monetary system may exist in various forms, and can not be, by any means, considered as establishing the double standard in such country. As a rule, the one metal or the other always asserted its supremacy in trade. The coins of the country were manufactured from the metal that did, and the other metal, as well as billon, or copper, was associated with the principal coins by the States endowing it with a payment power to a nominal value superior to its market value. Overvaluations of this kind sometimes occurred in the case of gold coins, but, as a rule, silver served as a representative of credit money, and was issued sometimes as divisional coins of limited legal-tender power, and sometimes as full legal tender. When issued, however, as full legal tender, the legal ratio of value always proved ineffectual if the manufacture of the under-value money was very large, because the under-value money became, in ordinary trade, the universally-accepted medium of exchange and measure of value, and the gold coins, as well as the large silver coins, whose value had not been debased, acquired an increased current value; in other words, they were at a premium.

After the end of the seventeenth century, gold began to obtain supremacy in England, and France commenced to accumulate a large amount of that metal. The system existing in countries with a mixed currency of gold and silver from the sixteenth to the end of the eighteenth century was not the double-standard system as understood in our day, but a system of parallel standard; that is, a system in which gold and silver coins circulated on an equality, but with no fixed legal ratio between the two metals as in the double-standard system. Contracts were concluded partly in gold and partly in silver money, or the use of the one kind of money or the other in certain transactions had been fixed by long-continued custom. As at that time, in consequence of the debasement of the coins, in payments which were not required to be immediately made, agreements on the coins to be received by the creditor were usual, the parallel system of valuation was no great impediment to trade. Even when the value of coins of the one metal was regulated legally in terms of the other, the rise of the rate of exchange of the better metal could not be prevented. Still, legislative attempts were frequently made after the beginning of the sixteenth century to arrest the rise of the value of gold coins.

The principles of the double standard, says Professor Lexis, first found legal expression and the real double standard was first adopted in the United States by the act of the 2d of April, 1792. As already remarked, that act expressly provides that:

1. The proportional value of gold and silver in all coins which shall by law be current as money within the United States shall be as fifteen to one, according to quantity and weight of pure gold and silver; that is to say, every fifteen pounds weight pure silver shall be of equal value in all payments with one pound weight of pure gold.

2. That all the gold and silver coins which shall have been struck at and issued from the mint shall be lawful tender in all payments whatsoever.

3. That it shall be lawful for any person or persons to bring to the said mint gold and silver bullion, and that the bullion so brought shall be there assayed and coined, as speedily as may be, and that free of expense to the person or persons by whom the same shall have been brought: *Provided, nevertheless*, That it shall be at the mutual option of the party or parties bringing such bullion and of the Director of the Mint to make an immediate exchange of coins for standard bullion with a deduction of one-half per cent from the weight of the pure gold or pure silver contained in the said bullion, as an indemnification to the mint for the time which will be necessarily required for coining the said bullion and for the advance which shall have been made in coins.

MONETARY LEGISLATION. 79

These three characteristics, a legal ratio of value between the two metals, unlimited legal-tender power of the coins of both, and unlimited coinage of them either gratis or with a mint charge to cover the actual cost of manufacture, must be considered necessary to the existence of the double standard, properly so called. If the coins of the one metal are made unlimited legal tender at a fixed legal ratio, while the coinage of those of the other is limited, or can not be effected on individual account, the double standard does not exist, but rather the "limping standard," or better, the "limping double standard."

Now, the United States act of April 2, 1792, was the first that introduced these three distinguishing marks into the monetary system of any country. Hence the contention that the double standard proper was first adopted by the United States by virtue of law.

The system established by the act of April 2, 1792, worked well for a time, although the ratio adopted soon became unfavorable to gold, which began and continued to be exported or hoarded until there was little or no gold in circulation in the United States.

The ratio of value between gold and silver recommended by Hamilton, viz., 1 to 15, corresponded very closely with the price of silver in London at the time, but shortly after the first coinages at the United States mint gold began slowly to rise. Up to 1806, however, the coinage of the country was mainly gold. This was doubtless partly due to the fact that the trade on the Lower Mississippi caused a continual influx of doubloons. The largest silver coinage during this period (1792–1806) was in 1799 ($423,515), and the gold coinage reached its maximum in 1802, when it amounted to $423,310. From 1806 to 1834 the coinage of silver preponderated. It could not be otherwise, because in Europe the ratio in coinage of gold and silver was between 15½ and 16. Still there was, in 1820, a coinage of $1,319,030 in gold against $501,680 in silver.

An ounce of gold purchasing only 15 ounces of silver in the United States, while in Europe it was worth 15½ or 16, gold was undervalued in the United States and naturally flowed to those countries in which it could command 15½ or 16 ounces of silver instead of 15. The greater part of the gold coinage for the United States after 1820 went to England, where, owing to the English resumption act passed in 1819, there was then a great demand for that metal, but not simply in exchange for silver at the nominal par value in the United States, for in the twenties the gold dollar reached a premium of about 5 per cent. as compared with the silver dollar, and the comparatively large coinage of gold in the years just preceding the amendment of the law of April 2, 1792, can be accounted for only by this premium. The coinages were:

Year.	Gold.	Silver.
1830	$643,105	$2,495,400
1831	714,270	3,175,600
1832	798,435	2,579,000
1833	978,550	2,759,000

The prevalence of the ratio of 1 : 15½ in Europe and the exportation of gold from the United States was promoted by the monetary legislation of France in the early part of this century. The ratio of gold to silver in France, about the time that Hamilton wrote his report on the establishment of a mint, was 1 to 14⅞, or, according to M. Gauden, Minister of Finances, 1 to 15. A message addressed to the Council of Five Hundred, in 1796, favored the ratio of 1 to 16, with the power to subsequently modify that proportion according to the variations of the market value of gold; but the proposition was rejected. Gauden finally succeeded in 1803 in having the future monetary system of France based on the mintage of both metals, with a ratio of 1 to 15½ and the free coinage of both gold and silver. The adoption by France of the ratio of 1 to 15½ was in flat contradiction with the monetary legislation of the United States, whose ratio corresponded to a price of silver of 62⅜ pence per ounce standard, while that of France corresponded to one of 60⅜ pence. Although at this time it was not as easy as it would be now to turn this difference of 2 pence, equivalent to about 3 per cent., to account by way of arbitrage, and although such operations were not then as frequent as at present, this divergence occasionally caused serious disturbances in our monetary system, and was pointed out as an element of danger in the aggregate monetary operations between the two countries. As trade developed and commercial intercourse between France and the United States assumed larger proportions, the United States began to feel the consequences of this divergent ratio by a loss of a large portion of the gold coins which were exported to France. A profitable difference between the mint and market ratios in the United States began to appear as early as 1810, and the money brokers were not slow to take advantage of it. Benton claims that there was no gold in the United States in 1812. This was not the case, but it is certain that there was very little in the twenties.

The causes of the loss of its gold and the means to be adopted to prevent it in the future were the cause of much discussion in the United States.

John Quincy Adams, Secretary of State, in his report on weights and measures, prepared in conformity with a resolution of the Senate of March 3, 1817, and submitted to that body February 22, 1821, questioned the correctness of the data on which Hamilton had based his reckoning in 1791.

Two years after the passage of the Senate resolution of March 3, 1817, *i. e.*, on March 1, 1819, the Secretary of the Treasury was asked by the House of Representatives to report such measures as might be expedient to procure and retain a sufficient quantity of gold and silver coin in circulation in the United States. In his report, Secretary Crawford stated that from the beginning of the war of 1812 until the suspension of specie payment in the United States in 1814 a large amount of specie was taken out of the United States by the sale of Government bills at a discount, Respecting the ratio of value between gold and silver, Secretary Crawford's report says:

> The relative value of gold and silver has been differently established in different nations. It has been different in the same nation at different periods. In England, an ounce of gold is equal in value to about 15.2 ounces of silver. In France, it is equal to 15.5, and, in Spain and Portugal, to 16 ounces. In the United States, an ounce of gold is equal to 15 ounces of silver. But the relative value of these metals in the markets, frequently differs from that assigned to them by the laws of the different civilized States. It is believed that gold, when compared with silver, has been for many years appreciating in value; and now, everywhere, commands in the money markets, a higher value than that which has been assigned to it in States where its relative value is greatest. If this is correct no injustice will result from a change in the relative legal value of gold and silver, so as to make it correspond with their relative marketable value. If gold, in relation to silver, should be raised 5 per cent., one ounce of it would be equal to 15.75 or 15¾ ounces of pure silver. This augmentation of its value would cause it to be imported in quantities sufficient to perform all the functions of currency. As it is not used to any considerable extent as a primary article of commerce, the fluctuations to which the silver currency is subject from that cause, would not affect it. It would be exported only when the rate of exchange against the country should exceed the expense of exportation. In ordinary circumstances, such a state of exchange would not be of long continuance. If the currency of the United States must, of necessity, continue to be paper, convertible into specie, an increase of the gold coinage, upon principles which shall afford the least inducement to exportation, is probably the most wholesome corrective that can be applied, after the rigid enforcement of that convertibility.

In the report made to the House of Representatives under date of March 17, 1832, by Mr. C. P. White, from the Select Committee of the House of Representatives on Coins, it was claimed "that there was no export of gold from the United States of consequence from 1792 to 1821, and that there was no indication that gold was rated too low in the United States standard of 1 to 15 earlier than 1821," when the English demand commenced.

The report of the Committee on the Currency transmitted

to the House of Representatives on the 2d of February, 1821, stated in opposition to this:

* * * * * * * * *

That they are of opinion that the value of American Gold compared with silver, ought to be somewhat higher than by law at present established.

On inquiry they find that gold coins, both foreign and of the United States, have, in a great measure, disappeared; and from the best calculation that can be made there is reason to apprehend they will be wholly banished from circulation, and it ought not to be a matter of surprise, under our present regulations, that this should be the case.

* * * * * * * * *

There have been coined at the Mint in the United States nearly six millions of dollars in gold.

It is doubtful whether any considerable portion of it can at this time be found within the United States.

It is ascertained * * * that the gold coin, in an office of discount and deposit of the Bank of the United States * * * in November 1819, amounted to $165,000 and the silver coin * * * to $118,000. That since that time, the silver coin has increased to $700,000, while the gold coin has diminished to * * * $1,200, one hundred only of which is American. * * *

* * * * * * * * *

There is proof positive that, although the ratio between gold and silver, provided for by the act of April 2, 1792, was very nearly the actual commercial ratio at the time and the exact commercial ratio one year after its passage, it soon departed from the market ratio, and in some years, as in 1808 and 1812, exceeded 1 to 16.

The commercial ratio of gold to silver from 1791 to 1834, as calculated by Dr. Soetbeer, was:

Year.	Ratio.	Year.	Ratio.	Year.	Ratio.	Year.	Ratio.	Year.	Ratio.
1791	15.05	1800	15.68	1809	15.96	1818	15.35	1827	15.74
1792	15.17	1801	15.46	1810	15.77	1819	15.33	1828	15.78
1793	15.00	1802	15.26	1811	15.53	1820	15.62	1829	15.78
1794	15.37	1803	15.41	1812	16.11	1821	15.95	1830	15.82
1795	15.55	1804	15.41	1813	16.25	1822	15.80	1831	15.72
1796	15.65	1805	15.79	1814	15.04	1823	15.84	1832	15.73
1797	15.41	1806	15.52	1815	15.26	1824	15.82	1833	15.93
1798	15.59	1807	15.43	1816	15.28	1825	15.70	1834	15.73
1799	15.74	1808	16.08	1817	15.11	1826	15.76		

But the disappearance of gold from the United States, under the operations of the act of 1792, was not the only monetary evil from which the country suffered at this time. The silver coins stamped at the Mint of the United States were also rapidly leaving the country, being expelled by foreign silver coins. The act of 1792 provided that each dollar should be of the value of a Spanish milled dollar, the same as then current. There were more Spanish milled dollars than dollars coined in the United States in circulation, and as they were heavier than the latter they commanded a premium. The natural result of this was an inducement to hoard the foreign pieces and coin United States dollars. The lighter United States dollars were exported to the West Indies and other places where they were received at their nominal value, on an equality with Spanish dollars. These were imported into the United States, recoined, and a profit realized on the operation. Whenever the banks were called upon for silver for exportation they paid out United States dollars, "This process," says Professor Laughlin, "kept the Mint busy, without the effect of filling the circulation with our own coins. The Mint, therefore, was a useless expense to the nation, but source of profit to the money brokers."

On this account, and to prevent the exchange of United States silver dollars for foreign silver pieces, President Jefferson ordered the suspension of the coinage of silver dollar pieces in the following note, addressed by Madison, then Secretary of State, to the Director of the Mint, at Philadelphia:

DEPARTMENT OF STATE, *May 1, 1806.*

SIR: In consequence of a representation from the director of the Bank of the United States that considerable purchases have been made of dollars coined at the Mint for the purpose of exporting them, and as it is probable further purchases and exportations will be made, the President directs that all the silver to be coined at the Mint shall be of small denominations, so that the value of the largest pieces shall not exceed half a dollar.

I am, etc., JAMES MADISON.
ROBERT PATTERSON, ESQ.,
Director of the Mint.

After the issuance of this order no silver dollar pieces were stamped for thirty years. But notwithstanding the discontinuance of the coinage of silver dollars, half dollars, two of which contained as much fine metal as a dollar piece, continued to be coined and exported. Spanish dollars were imported, being exchanged against American half dollars, which went out. Up to 1830 $34,000,000 of silver coins of all denominations had been coined by the United States Mint, only $14,000,000 of which, it was estimated, remained in the country. The Spanish pieces which had been substituted for United States pieces suffered greatly from abrasion. They had lost much in weight, and this, too, contributed to the expulsion from circulation of American coins. The evil had grown to such dimensions that a memorial of the New York bankers, led by Mr. Gallatin in 1834, represented:

> That the dollar of Spain and the gold and silver coins of the United States constitute at present the only legal currency of the country; and that, from the commercial value of the Spanish dollar and the intrinsic value of gold coins of the United States, they have become mere articles of merchandise and are no longer to be considered as forming any portion of the metallic currency.

From the discussions on the coinage previous to the passage of the act supplementary to the "act establishing a mint and regulating the coins of the United States," of April 2, 1792, extracts from two reports (he made three altogether) of Mr. Campbell P. White, of New York, are here given, because they contain some of the most significant utterances in the currency controversy of the times, containing as they do a confirmation from experience of recognized principles of monetary science. In the first report of 1831 Mr. White says:

> That there are inherent and incurable defects in the system which regulates the standard of value of both gold and silver; its instability as a measure of contracts and mutability as the practical currency of a particular nation are serious imperfections, while the impossibility of maintaining both metals in concurrent, simultaneous, or promiscuous circulation appears to be as clearly ascertained.
> That the standard being fixed in one metal is the nearest approach to invariableness, and precludes the necessity of further legislative interference.

In the report of 1832 he says:

If both metals are preferred, the like relative proportion of the aggregate amount of metallic currency will be possessed, *subject to frequent changes from gold to silver* and *vice versa*, according to the variations in the relative value of these metals. The committee think that the *desideratum in the monetary system is the standard of uniform value;* they can not ascertain that both metals have ever circulated simultaneously, concurrently, and indiscriminately in any country where there are banks or money dealers, and they entertain the conviction that the nearest approach to an invariable standard is its establishment *in one metal*, which metal shall compose exclusively the currency for large payments.

THE GOLD PERIOD, 1834–1853—ACTS OF JUNE 28, 1834, AND JANUARY 18, 1837.

The final result of the protracted discussion of the changes which time and experience had shown must be made in the monetary system of the United States, established by the act of April 2, 1792, was the passage of the act of June 28, 1834. (4 Stat. L., p. 699.)

The text of that act is as follows:

AN ACT concerning the gold coins of the United States, and for other purposes.

Be it enacted by the Senate and House of Representatives of the United States of America, in Congress assembled, That the gold coins of the United States shall contain the following quantities of metal, that is to say: each eagle shall contain two-hundred and thirty-two grains of pure gold, and two hundred and fifty-eight grains of standard gold; each half-eagle one hundred and sixteen grains of pure gold, and one hundred and twenty-nine grains of standard gold; each quarter-eagle shall contain fifty-eight grains of pure gold, and sixty-four and a half grains of standard gold; every such eagle shall be of the value of ten dollars; every such half eagle shall be of the value of five dollars; and every such quarter eagle shall be of the value of two dollars and fifty cents; and the said gold coins shall be receivable in all payments, when of full weight, according to their respective values; and when of less than full weight, at less values, proportioned to their respective actual weights.

SEC. 2. *And be it further enacted,* That all standard gold or silver deposited for coinage arter the thirty-first of July next, shall be paid for in coin, under the direction of the Secretary of the Treasury, within five days from the making of such deposit, deducting from the amount of said deposit of gold or silver one-half per centum: *Provided,* That no deduction shall be made unless said advance be required by such depositor within forty days.

SEC. 3. *And be it further enacted,* That all gold coins in the United States, minted anterior to thirty-first day of July next, shall be receivable in all payments at the rate of ninty-four and eight-tenths of a cent per pennyweight.

MONETARY LEGISLATION. 87

SEC. 4. *And be it further enacted*, That the better to secure a conformity of the said gold coins to their respective standards as aforesaid, from every separate mass of standard gold, which shall be made into coins at the said Mint, there shall be taken, set apart by the Treasurer and reserved in his custody, a certain number of pieces, not less than three, and that once in every year the pieces so set apart and reserved shall be assayed under the inspection of the officers, and at the time, and in the manner now provided by law, and, if it shall be found that the gold so assayed, shall not be inferior to the said standard hereinbefore declared more than one part in three hundred and eighty-four in fineness, and one part in five hundred in weight, the officer or officers of the said Mint whom it may concern, shall be held excusable; but if any greater inferiority shall appear, it shall be certified to the President of the United States, and if he shall so decide, the said officer or officers shall be hereafter disqualified to hold their respective offices: *Provided*, That if, in making any delivery of coin at the Mint in payment of a deposit, the weight thereof shall be found defective, the officer concerned shall be responsible to the owner for the full weight, if claimed at the time of delivery.

SEC. 5. *And be it further enacted*, That this act shall be in force from and after the thirty-first day of July, in the year one thousand eight hundred and thirty-four.

Approved, June 28, 1834.

The act of June 28, 1834, it will be noticed, changed the ratio of gold to silver from $1:15$ to $1:16$ (15.988) by reducing the weight of the fine gold in the gold coins to 23.20 grains Troy.

An act approved January 18, 1837, changed the weight of the fine gold in the gold coins to 23.22 grains, and the fineness from 0.899225 to 0.900. Both the acts of 1834 and that of 1837 left the fine weight of the silver dollar unaltered. Its standard weight, however, was lowered from 416 to 412½ grains.

The act of 1834 provided for a mint ratio, $1:16$, in which silver was undervalued as gold had been undervalued in that of 1792. The result was that thereafter silver was expelled from circulation, as gold had been before.

Up to 1847, however, the variation of the legal ratio established in 1834, from the commercial, was not great enough to allow the coinages of gold in the United States to preponderate to any very marked extent over the silver coinages, although gold flowed to the mint to an amount four times as large as in 1833. It is noteworthy that after the year 1801 our silver coinage consisted almost exclusively of half dollars, and that comparatively few dollar pieces were stamped. The silver half dollars were full legal tender and this fact assimilated them to the dollar pieces, two of them containing exactly the same amount of fine silver as the 1-dollar piece. While the fractional dollar pieces were thus coined, the United States possessed the double standard proper, in the full sense of the term. But the existence of the double standard in the United States could exercise no great influence outside of it because the amounts of both metals coined were rather small.

Not until 1847 did the coinage of gold assume any very great dimensions. In that year and before the Californian discoveries it amounted to $20,202,325, but fell in 1848 to $3,775,513.

The effect of the Californian discoveries on the ratio of value of the two metals was first felt in 1850, and the coinage of silver began to decrease. The turning point was reached in 1853; the coinages of silver rose rapidly, but simply because, by the act of February 21 of that year, half dollars, quarter dollars, dimes, and half dimes (in the ratio value of 1 : 14.88 as compared with gold) were made legal tender to the amount of only $5, and a larger amount of them had to be coined. It has been already remarked that it was an error to provide, as the act of 1792 had done, that the subsidiary silver coins—that is, those of a denomination below one dollar—should have a weight and fineness corresponding to that of the dollar piece, and that they should have the same legal tender power as the latter, for it subsequently led to the disappearance of all silver coins used for small change. When 371¼ grains of fine silver came to be worth more than one dollar in gold, 2 half dollars or 4 quarter dollars or 10 dimes or 20 half dimes came to be worth the same sum, and there was as large a profit in exchanging subsidiary silver coins as dollar pieces for gold, so that the former were expelled from circulation, the business of the country was much hampered by the lack of fractional coins, and the United States began to lose not only its silver dollar pieces but its silver fractional currency.

GOLD PERIOD, 1853-1873—DEMONETIZATION OF SILVER BY THE ACT OF FEBRUARY 21, 1853.

In 1850 the United States had practically the single gold standard and not enough of fractional silver for the requirements of retail trade.

The act of February 21, 1853, remedied this evil as was said above by providing that from and after the 1st of June, 1853, the weight of the half dollar should be 192 grains, and the quarter dollar, dime, and half dime, should be, respectively, one-half, one-fifth, and one-tenth of the weight of the half dollar, and that the subsidiary silver coins, issued in conformity with the above provisions should be legal tender in in payment of debts for all sums not exceeding $5.

The passage of the act of 1853 was, to say the least, an impairment of the double standard in the United States. Taken in connection with the changing of the legal ratio from 1:15 to about 1:16 in 1834, it was intended to place the country, de facto, on the single-gold standard, and there were those openly avowed that such was its aim. Hon. Cyrus L. Dunham. of Indiana, a member of the Committee of Ways and Means of the House of Representatives, said:

Another objection urged against this proposed change is that it gives us a standard of gold only.................What advantage is to be obtained by a standard of the two metals, which is not as well, if not much better, attained by a single standard, I am unable to perceive; while there are very great disadvantages resulting from it, as the experience of every nation which has attempted to maintain it has proved. Indeed, it is utterly impossible that you should long at a time maintain a double standard............ ......Gentlemen talk about a double standard of gold and silver as a thing that exists and that we propose to change. *We have had but a single standard for the last three or four years. That has been and now is gold. We promise to let it remain so, and to adopt silver to it, to regulate it by it.*

In answer to another plan the same speaker says:—

> We would thereby still continue the double standard of gold and silver, a thing the committee desire to obviate. *They desire to have the standard currency to consist of gold only,* and that these silver coins shall be entirely subservient to it and that they shall be used rather as tokens than as standard currency. (See Congressional Globe, Appendix, second session Thirty-second Congress, p. 190.)

The act of 1834, establishing the legal ratio of 1:16, had, as already remarked, undervalued silver. The average commercial ratio of the two metals did not approach very closely to this legal ratio until 1873, when it was 1:15.92, and 1874, when it reached 1:16.17. In 1833 the commercial ratio very nearly coincided with the United States legal ratio, having been 1:15.93, a figure to which it did not again approximate until 1845, when it was 1:15.92. After this the ratio rapidly changed to the disadvantage of gold. It was in 1846, 1:15.90; 1847, 1:15.80; in 1848, 1:15.85; in 1849, 1:15.78; in 1850, 1:15.70; in 1851, 1:15.46; in 1852, 1:15.33. The depreciation of gold evidenced by these figures was, especially after 1849, due to the discoveries of gold in California and Australia. From an annual average production in 1840 to 1850 of about $38,000,000 the gold supply increased to over $150,000,000 after 1850. The natural effect of this increase was to lower the value of gold. If the gold and silver coins of the United States were both to be kept in circulation, a new adjustment of the legal ratio to the market ratio was necessary; but as no effort was made to effect such a new adjustment in the legislation of 1853, it must be inferred that the framers of the act of February 21, of that year, had no desire to keep silver any longer in circulation, and that they drafted it in such a manner that gold alone would be retained, with silver as subsidiary coin. The exportation of silver was heaviest between 1848 and 1851, for the value of silver was then greatest as compared with gold.

The act of February 21 was a step in the direction of the gold standard. No reference was made in it whatever to the silver dollar. The reason is that it had not been in circulation for years. Up to 1853 less than four million standard silver dollars had been coined in the United States, and of these scarcely any were still in circulation. There was, on the other hand, an abundance of gold, consequent on the discoveries in California and the overvaluation of the metal in the mint ratio. The change in the standard implied in the act was regarded by the people with indifference, if indeed they noticed it at all.

The framers of the law, on the other hand, knew full well what they were doing, as is shown by this utterance of the chairman of the House Committee on Ways and Means:

> We intend to do what the best writers on political economy have approved; what experience, where the experiment has been tried, has demonstrated to be necessary and proper—to make but one standard of currency and to make all others subservient to it. We mean to make gold the standard coin, and to make these new coins applicable and convenient, not for large, but for small trnnsactions.

It thus happens that the real demonetization of silver in the United States took place in 1853. Its demonetization in 1873 was only nominal. Nor was its demonetization in 1853, as has just been shown, the result of accident or an oversight. It was deliberate and intentional. The act of 1873 only conformed the law to the actual monetary condition, so far as the metallic currency of the United States was concerned, that had existed here for nearly a quarter of a century anterior to its passage.

The experience of the country since 1792 had demonstrated that under a bimetallic system, with a fixed legal ratio between the two metals, the one undervalued in the coinage disappeared from circulation and was thus practically demonetized, and it was logically inferred by the advocates of a gold standard in 1853 that by undervaluing silver in the ratio of 1 : 16 silver would disappear and leave the country with legal-tender currency composed of gold only. In this connection Professor Laughlin says:

It was in 1853 that Congress, judging from our past experience and that of other countries, came to the conclusion that a double standard was an impossibility for any length of time.

It cannot be said, however, that this conclusion was reached wholly through unselfish reasons. The underlying prejudice in favor of gold, if gold can be had, which we are sure to find deeply seated in the desires of our business community whenever occasion gives it an opportunity for display, was here manifesting itself. The country found itself with a single metal in circulation. Had that metal been silver, we should have had to chronicle again the grumbling dissertations on the disappearance of gold which characterized the period preceding 1834. But in 1853 the single standard was gold. This was a situation which one rebelled against. Indeed, no one seemed to regard it as anything else than good fortune (except so far as the subsidiary coins had disappeared). It was very much as if a ranchman, starting with 100 good cattle and 100 inferior ones, had found when branding time came, that, by virtue of exchange with his neighbors, the 200 cattle assigned to him were, in his judgment, all good ones and none inferior. From a selfish point of view he had no reason to complain. It would have been a very different story had the 200 cattle all been inferior.

In the debate it was proposed that, as the cause of the change in the relative values of gold and silver was the increased product of gold, the proper remedy should be to increase the quantity of gold in the gold coins. This was exactly the kind of treatment which should have been adopted in regard to silver in 1834, and it seems quite reasonable that this should have been the only true and just policy in 1853. Certainly it was, if it was intended to bring the mint ratio into accord with the market ratio and try again the experiment of a double standard. But this was exactly what Congress chose to abandon. There was no discussion as to how a readjustment of the ratio between the two metals might be reached, for it was already decided that only one metal was to be retained. This decision, consequently, carried us to a point where a ratio between the two metals was not of the slightest concern. And so it remained. The United States had no thought about the ratios between gold and silver thereafter until the extraordinary fall in the value of silver in 1876. The policy of the United States in retaining gold, once that it was in circulation, was only doing a little earlier what France did in later years. When the cheapened gold, after 1850, had filled the channels of circulation in France and had driven out silver, France made no objections; but when a subsequent change in silver tended to drive out the gold France quietly held on to her gold. The United States, as well as France again showed the unconscious preference of gold of which Hamilton spoke in 1792.

In the provisions of the act of 1853 nothing whatever was said as to the silver-dollar piece. It had entirely disappeared from circulation years before, and acquiescence in its absence was everywhere found. No attempt whatever was thereafter made to change the legal ratio in order that both metals might again be brought into concurrent circulation. Having enough gold, the country did not care for silver. At the existing and only nominal mint ratio of 1 : 16 the silver dollar could not circulate, and no attempt was made in the act to bring it into circulation. It is, therefore, to be kept distinctly in mind that in 1853 the actual use of silver as an unlimited legal tender equally with gold was decisively abandoned. Under any conditions then existing a double standard was publicly admitted to be hopeless. The main animus of the act, therefore, is to be found in what is not included in it—that is, in the omission to insert any provision which would bring again the silver dollar into circulation.

As the act stands on the statute books it is practically nothing more than a regulation of the subsidiary silver coinage, and its study is but a lesson in the proper principles which should regulate that part of a metallic currency.

THE LEGAL-TENDER NOTES.

Before dwelling on the act of February 12, 1873, it is necessary to call attention to the issue of the legal-tender notes, commonly called "greenbacks," and to the national-bank notes issued during and since the civil war, as they constitute no small portion of the circulating medium of the United States.

First, as to the United States legal-tender notes. The first non-interest-bearing legal-tender notes were authorized by an act of February 12, 1862, and were dated March 10, 1862. There was printed on their backs: "This note is a legal tender for all debts, public and private, except duties or imposts, and interest on the public debt, and is exchangeable for United States 6 per cent. bonds, redeemable at the pleasure of the United States after five years." On June 7, 1862, the Secretary of the Treasury recommended a further issue of $150,000,000 of legal-tender notes. A bill authorizing this issue was signed by the President on June 11, 1862. The act of March 3, 1863, authorized the issue of an additional $150,000,000 of legal-tender notes. The aggregate issue was $450,000,000. The highest amount of legal-tender notes outstanding at any one time was on January 3, 1864, when it reached $449,338,902.

In his report for 1865, Secretary McCulloch expressed the opinion that the legal-tender acts were war measures, and ought not to remain in force one day longer than should be necessary to enable the people to prepare for a return to the gold standard. During the same month Congress passed a resolution, by a vote 144 against 6, "cordially concurring in the views of the Secretary of the Treasury in relation to the contraction of the currency with a view to as early a resumption of specie payments as the business interests of the country will permit." An act approved March 12, 1866, authorized the retirement and cancellation of not more than ten millions of legal-tender notes within six months from the passage of the act. Under this act the amount outstanding was so far reduced that on December 31, 1867, the amount was $356,000,000. Between that date and January 15, 1874, the amount was increased to $382,979,815, and on June 20, 1874, the maximum amount was fixed at $382,000,000. Section 3 of the act of January 14, 1875, authorized the increase of the circulation of national banks, but required the Secretary of the Treasury to retire legal-tender notes to an amount equal to 80 per cent. of the national-bank notes thereafter issued, until the amount of the legal-tender notes outstanding should be $300,000,000 and no more. Under this act $35,318,984 of legal-tender notes were retired, leaving the amount in circulation on May 31, 1878, when the act was repealed, $346,681,016, at which figure the amount outstanding has since remained, that act providing that from and after its passage it should not be lawful for the Secretary of the Treasury, or other officers under him, to cancel or retire any more of the United States legal-tender notes, and that when any of said notes might be redeemed or received into the Treasury from any source whatever, and should belong to the United States, they should not be cancelled or retired, but should be reissued and paid out again and kept in circulation.

The act of February 14, 1875, had authorized the Secretary of the Treasury, on and after January 1, 1879, to redeem in coin the legal-tender notes on their presentation at the office of the assistant treasurer in the city of New York, in sums of not less than $50, and empowered him, for that purpose, "to use any surplus revenue from time to time, in the Treasury, not otherwise appropriated, and to issue, sell, and dispose of, at not less than par in coin, the 5 and 4 per cent. bonds authorized by the act of July 14, 1870." On January 1, 1879, the Secretary held $135,000,000 in gold coin and bullion, and over $32,000,000 in silver coin and bullion, the gold coin alone being equal to 40 per cent. of the United States notes then outstanding. The banks of the country, at the date of resumption, held more than one-third of the outstanding Treasury notes; but they had so much confidence in the ability of the Secretary to maintain resumption that they presented none for redemption. As, therefore, there was no demand for payment of the notes of the Government, the gold coin in the Treasury, which amounted to $135,000,000 on the day of resumption, increased more than $36,000,000 in the next ten months.

The following table shows the amount of the gold reserve for the redemption of legal-tender notes at the end of the fiscal years named:

STATEMENT SHOWING THE AMOUNT OF GOLD IN THE TREASURY, GOLD CERTIFICATES IN CIRCULATION, AND NET GOLD IN THE TREASURY AT THE CLOSE OF EACH FISCAL YEAR FROM JUNE 30, 1879, TO JUNE 30, 1895.

Year.	Total gold in Treasury.	Gold certificates in circulation.	Net gold in Treasury.
1879	$135,236,475	$15,279,820	$119,956,655
1880	126,145,427	7,693,900	118,181,527
1881	163,171,061	5,759,520	157,411,541
1882	148,506,390	5,020,020	143,486,370
1883	198,078,568	59,807,370	138,271,198
1884	204,876,594	71,146,640	133,729,954
1885	247,028,625	126,729,730	120,298,895
1886	232,554,886	76,044,375	156,510,511
1887	277,979,654	91,225,437	186,754,217
1888	314,704,822	121,094,650	193,610,172
1889	303,504,319	116,792,759	186,711,560
1890	331,612,423	131,380,019	190,232,404
1891	238,518,122	120,850,399	117,667,723
1892	255,577,705	141,235,339	114,342,366
1893	188,455,433	92,970,019	95,485,414
1894	131,217,434	66,344,409	64,873,025
1895	155,893,931	48,381,569	107,512,362

THE NATIONAL BANK NOTES.

Next in importance, as well as in the order of time of their issuance, to the legal-tender notes of the United States, in the paper-money currency of the country, come the national-bank notes. The first national bank act was approved February 25, 1863, which act was repealed and superseded by the act of similar title approved June 3, 1864, with little change in its leading features. The latter act, section 21, provided that upon the transfer and delivery of United States bonds to the Treasurer of the United States, as required by section 20 of the act, a national bank association should receive from the Comptroller of the Currency circulating notes of different denominations equal in amount to 90 per cent. of the amount of said bonds at the par value thereof. By section 22 it was enacted that the entire amount of notes for circulation to be issued under the act should not exceed $300,000,000. This amount was subsequently increased by law. The largest amount of national-bank notes outstanding was in January, 1883, when it rose to $362,651,169, and the lowest in July, 1891, when it had declined to $167,927,574. In December, 1894, it was $207,472,603, and on November 1, 1895, $207,364,028.

GOLD PERIOD, 1873-1878—DEMONETIZATION OF SILVER IN 1873.

On the 25th of April, 1870, the Secretary of the Treasury transmitted a bill to Congress providing for the revision of the coinage laws of the United States. It was considered for five sessions of Congress and was finally passed and became a law February 12, 1873.

It provided that the gold coins of the United States should be a 1-dollar piece. which at the standard weight of 25.8 grains should be the unit of value; a 3-dollar piece, a 5-dollar piece, a 10-dollar piece, and a 20-dollar piece of a standard weight, proportional to the 1-dollar piece, and that such coins should be a legal tender in all payments at their nominal value when not below the standard weight and limit of tolerance. It also provided that the silver coins of the United States should be a trade dollar, a half dollar, a quarter dollar, and a dime; that the weight of the half dollar should be 12½ grams, and that of the quarter dollar and dime proportional thereto. The weight of the trade dollar was fixed at 420 grains Troy. All these coins were made legal tender to the amount of $5. Section 21 of the act provided that any owner of silver bullion might deposit the same at any mint, to be formed into bars, or into dollars of the weight of 420 grains Troy, designated in the act as trade dollars, and that no deposit of silver for other coinage should be received. The bill met with little opposition either in the Senate or in the House of Representatives. The silver dollars previously coined, of which there were but few in existence, maintained their quality as legal tender, but the coinage of new full legal-tender dollars, whether on Government or private account, was discontinued. This act was the logical complement of the legislation of 1853.

HON. JOHN SHERMAN ADVOCATES THE SINGLE GOLD STANDARD, WITH SILVER AS LIMITED LEGAL TENDER.

There was at first complete acquiescence in the result of the legislation of 1873, as there had been in that of 1853, and not until the decline of silver in 1875 and 1876 were any suggestions made for the coinage anew of silver dollars, although in both those years the currency of the country was inconvertible paper, and no gold or silver coins were in circulation. A large number of silver bills were introduced in the House of Representatives in the summer of 1876. The agitation in and out of Congress in favor of the coinage of silver dollars continued through 1877. Hon. John Sherman, then Secretary of the Treasury, refers to it in his report for 1877 in the following words, in which will be found a concise history of our monetary experience from 1792 until then:

The question of the issue of a silver dollar for circulation as money has been much discussed and carefully examined by a commission organized by Congress, which has recommended the coinage of the old silver dollar. With such legislative provision as will maintain its current value at par with gold, its issue is respectfully recommended. A gold coin of the denomination of one dollar is too small for convenient circulation, while such a coin in silver would be convenient for a multitude of daily transactions, and is in a form to satisfy the natural instinct of hoarding.

Of the metals, silver is of most general use for coinage. It is a part of every system of coinage even in countries where gold is the sole legal standard. It best measures the common wants of life, but, from its weight and bulk, is not a convenient medium in the larger exchanges of commerce. Its production is reasonably steady in amount. The relative market value of silver and gold is far more stable than that of any other two commodities, still it does vary. It is not in the power of human law to prevent the variation. This inherent difficulty has compelled all nations to adopt one or the other as the sole standard of value, or to authorize an alternative standard of either, or to coin both metals at an arbitrary standard and to maintain one at par with the other by limiting its amount and legal-tender quality and receiving or redeeming it at par with the other.

It has been the careful study of statesmen for many years to secure a bimetallic currency not subject to the changes of market value, and so adjusted that both kinds can be kept in circulation together, not alternating with each other. The growing tendency has been to adopt for coins the principle of " redeemability " applied to different forms of paper money. By limiting tokens, silver, and paper money to the amount needed for business, and promptly receiving or redeeming all that may at any time be in excess, all these forms of money can be kept in circulation, in large amounts, at par with gold. In this way tokens of inferior intrinsic value are readily circulated, but do not depreciate below the paper money into which they are convertible. The fractional silver coin now in circulation, though the silver of which it is composed is of less market value than the paper money, passes readily among all classes of people and answers all the purposes for which it was designed. *And so the silver dollar, if restored to our coinage, would greatly add to the convenience of the people. But this coin should be subject to the same rule, as to issue and convertibility, as other forms of money. If the market value of the silver in it were less than that of gold coin of the same denomination and it were issued in unlimited quantities, and made a legal tender for all debts, it would demonetize gold and depreciate our paper money.*

The importance of gold as the standard of value is conceded by all. Since 1834 it has been practically the sole coin standard of the United States, and since 1815 has been the sole standard of Great Britain. Germany has recently adopted the same standard. France and other Latin nations have suspended the coinage of silver, and, it is supposed, will gradually either adopt the sole standard of gold or provide for the convertibility of silver coin, on the demand of the holder, into gold coin.

In the United States several experiments have been made with the view of retaining both gold and silver in circulation. The Second Congress undertook to

MONETARY LEGISLATION. 99

establish the ratio of 15 of silver to 1 of gold, with free coinage of both metals. By this ratio gold was undervalued, as 1 ounce of gold was worth more in the markets of the world than 15 ounces of silver, and gold, therefore, was exported. To correct this, in 1837, the ratio was fixed at 16 to 1; but 16 ounces of silver were worth more than 1 ounce of gold, so that silver was demonetized.

These difficulties in the adjustment of gold and silver coinage were fully considered by Congress prior to the passage of the act approved February 21, 1853. By that act a new, and, it was believed, a permanent, policy was adopted to secure the simultaneous circulation of both silver and gold coins in the United States. Silver fractional coins were provided for at a ratio of 14.88 in silver to 1 in gold, and were only issued in exchange for gold coin. The right of private parties to deposit silver bullion for such coinage was repealed and these coins were issued for bullion purchased by the Treasurer of the Mint, and only upon the account and for the profit of the United States. The coin was a legal tender only in payment of debts for all sums not exceeding $5. Though the silver in this coin was worth in the market 3.13 cents on the dollar less than gold coin, yet its convenience for use as change, its issue by the Government only in exchange for, and its practical convertibility into, gold coin maintained it in circulation at par with gold coin. If the slight error in the ratio of 1792 prevented gold from entering into circulation for forty-five years, and the slight error in 1837 brought gold into circulation and banished silver until 1853, how much more certainly will an error now at 9 per cent. cause gold to be exported and silver to become the sole standard of value? Is it worth while to travel again the round of errors, when experience has demonstrated that both metals can only be maintained in circulation together by adhering to the policy of 1853?

The silver dollar was not mentioned in the act of 1853, but from 1792 until 1874 it was worth more in the market than the gold dollar provided for in the act of 1837. It was not a current coin contemplated as being in circulation at the passage of the act of February 12, 1873. The whole amount of such dollars issued prior to 1853 was $2,553,000. Subsequent to 1853, and until it was dropped from our coinage in 1873, the total amount issued was $5,492,838, or an aggregate of $8,045,838, and this was almost exclusively for exportation.

By the coinage act approved February 12, 1873, fractional silver coins were authorized, similar in general character to the coins of 1853, but with a slight increase of silver in them to make them conform exactly to the French coinage, and the old dollar was replaced by the trade dollar of 420 grains of standard silver.

Much complaint has been made that this was done with the design of depriving the people of the privilege of paying their debts in a cheaper money than gold, but it is manifest that this is an error. No one then did or could foresee the subsequent fall in the market value of silver. The silver dollar was an unknown coin to the people, and was not in circulation even on the Pacific Slope, where coin was in common use. The trade dollar of 420 grains was substituted for the silver dollar of 412½ grains because it was believed that it was better adapted to supersede the Mexican dollar in the Chinese trade, and experiment proved this to be true. Since the trade dollar was authorized $30,710,400 have been issued, or nearly four times the entire issue of old silver dollar since the foundation of the

Government. Had not the coinage act of 1873 passed, the United States would now be compelled to suspend the free coinage of silver dollars, as the Latin nations did, or to have silver as the sole coin standard of value.

Since February, 1873, great changes have occurred in the market value of silver. Prior to that time the silver in the old dollar was worth more than a gold dollar, while at present it is worth about 92 cents, If by law any holder of silver bullion might deposit it in the mint and demand a full legal-tender dollar for every $412\frac{1}{2}$ grains of standard silver deposited, the result would be inevitable that as soon as the mints could supply the demand, the silver dollar would, by a financial law as fixed and invariable as the law of gravitation, become the only standard of value. All forms of paper money would fall to that standard or below it, and gold would be demonetized and quoted at a premium equal to its value in the markets of the world. For a time the run to deposit bullion at the mint would give to silver an artificial value, of which the holders and producers of silver bullion would have the sole benefit. The utmost capacity of the mints would be employed for years to supply this demand at the cost of and without profit to the people. The silver dollar would take the place of gold as rapidly as coined, and be used in the payment of customs duties, causing the accumulation of such coins in the Treasury. If used in paying the interest on the public debt, the grave questions already presented would arise with public creditors, seriously affecting the public credit.

It is urged that the free coinage of silver in the United States would restore its market value to that of gold. Market value is fixed by the world, and not by the United States alone, and is affected by the whole mass of silver in the world. As the enormous and continuous demand for silver in Asia has not prevented the fall of silver, it is not likely that the limited demand for silver in this country, where paper money is now and will be the chief medium of exchange, will cause any considerable advance in its value. This advance, if any, will be secured by the demand for silver bullion for coin to be issued by and for the United States, as well as if it were issued for the benefit of the holder of the bullion. If the financial condition of our country is so grievous that we must at every hazard have a cheaper dollar in order to lessen the burden of debts already contracted, it is far better, rather than to adopt the single standard of silver, to boldly reduce the number of grains in the gold dollar or to abandon and retrace all efforts to make United States notes equal to coin. Either expedient will do greater harm to the public at large than any possible benefit to debtors.

The free coinage of silver will also impair the pledge made of the custom duties by the act of February, 1862, for the payment of the interest of the public debt. The policy thus far adhered to of collecting these duties in gold coin has been the chief cause of upholding and advancing the public credit and making it possible to lessen the burden of interest by the process of refunding.

In view of these considerations the Secretary has felt it to be his duty to earnestly urge upon Congress the serious objections to the free coinage of silver on such conditions as will demonetize gold, greatly disturb all the financial operations of the Government, suddenly revolutionize the basis of our currency, throw upon the Government the increased cost of coinage, arrest the refunding of the public debt, and impair the public credit, with no apparent advantage to the people at large.

The Secretary believes that all the beneficial results hoped for from a liberal issue of silver coin can be secured by issuing this coin, in pursuance of the general policy of the act of 1853, in exchange for United States notes, coined from bullion purchased in the open market by the United States, and maintaining it by redemption, or otherwise, at par with gold coin. *It could be made a legal tender for such sums and on such contracts as would secure it the most general circulation.* It could be easily redeemed in United States notes and gold coin, and only reissued when demanded for public convenience. If the essential qualitie of redeemability given to United States notes, bank bills, tokens, fractional coins, and currency maintains them at par, how much easier it would be to maintain the silver dollar of intrinsic market value, nearly equal to gold, at par with gold coin by giving to it the like quality of redeemability. To still further secure a fixed relative value of silver and gold, the United States might invite an international convention of commercial nations. Even such a convention, while it might check the fall of silver, could not prevent the operation of that higher law which places the market value of silver above human control. Issued upon the conditions here stated, the Secretary is of opinion that the silver dollar will be a great public advantage, but that if issued without limit, upon the demand of the owners of silver bullion, it will be a great public injury. (Annual Report of the Secretary of the Treasury on the State of the Finances, 1877.)

THE PERIOD OF THE LIMPING STANDARD, 1878 TO THE PRESENT TIME. ACTS OF 1878 AND 1890.

Notwithstanding the recommendations of the Secretary and the veto of the President, an act for the coinage of silver dollars to a limited amount was passed by Congress February 28, 1878. The material provisions of that act are as follows:

That there shall be coined, at the several mints of the United States, silver dollars of the weight of four hundred and twelve and a half grains troy of standard silver, as provided in the act of January eighteenth, eighteen hundred thirty-seven, on which shall be the devices and superscriptions provided by said act; which coins together with all silver dollars heretofore coined by the United States, of like weight and fineness, shall be a legal tender at their nominal value, for all debts and dues public and private, except where otherwise expressely stipulated in the contract. And the Secretary of the Treasury is authorized and directed to purchase, from time to time, silver bullion, at the market price thereof, not less than two million dollars worth per month, nor more than four million dollars worth per month, and cause the same to be coined monthly, as fast as so purchased, into such dollars; and a sum sufficient to carry out the foregoing provision of this act is hereby appropriated out of any money in the Treasury not otherwise appropriated. And any gain or seigniorage arising from this coinage shall be accounted for and paid into the Treasury, as provided under existing laws relative to the subsidiary coinage: *Provided*, That the amount of money at any one time invested in such silver bullion, exclusive of such resulting coin, shall not exceed five million dollars: *And provided further*, That nothing in this act shall be construed to authorize the payment in silver of certificates of deposit issued under the provisions of section two hundred and fifty-four of the Revised Statutes. * * *

SEC. 3. That any holder of the coin. authorized by this act may deposit the same with the Treasurer or any assistant treasurer of the United States, in sums not less than ten dollars, and receive therefor certificates of not less than ten dollars each, corresponding with the denominations of the United States notes. The coin deposited for or representing the certificates shall be retained in the Treasury for the payment of the same on demand. Said certificates shall be receivable for customs, taxes, and all public dues, and, when so received, may be reissued.

Under the act of 1878 the United States Government purchased a total of 291,018,018.56 ounces, fine, of silver, at a sost of $308,279,261.17, the average price per ounce being $1.0583. The coining value of the silver thus purchased was $376,265,722.

The act of 7878 was not entirely satisfactory to the advocates of silver. It had not conceded enough in favor of that metal. For nearly ten years the repeal of its purchasing clause was recommended by the Presidents in their messages and by the Secretaries of the Treasury in their reports. But while the Presidents and the Secretaries were pointing out the danger of the act to the monetary conditions of the country strong endeavors were being put forth in both Houses of Congress to find means to still further increase the coinage of silver. Efforts were made for a series of years to procure the passage of a bill providing for the free coinage of silver, but were unsuccessful. After much agitation and discussion, extending from the time of the passage of the act of 1878 until the middle of 1890, the act of July 14 of the latter year was approved by the President. It was a compromise measure between the adherents of the unlimited coinage of full legal-tender silver and their opponents.

The act of July 14, 1890, is here given:

MONETARY LEGISLATION.   103

AN ACT directing the purchase of silver bullion and the issue of Treasury notes thereon, and for other purposes.

Be it enacted by the Senate and House of Representatives of the United States of America in Congress assembled, That the Secretary of the Treasury is hereby directed to purchase, from time to time, silver bullion to the aggregate amount of four million five hundred thousand ounces, or so much thereof as may be offered in each month, at the market price thereof, not exceeding one dollar for three hundred and seventy-one and twenty-five hundredths grains of pure silver, and to issue in payment for such purchases of silver bullion Treasury notes of the United States to be prepared by the Secretary of the Treasury, in such forms and of such denominations, not less than one dollar nor more than one thousand dollars, as he may prescribe, and a sum sufficient to carry into effect the provisions of this act is hereby appropriated out of any money in the Treasury not otherwise appropriated.

SEC. 2. That the Treasury notes issued in accordance with the provisions of this act shall be redeemable on demand in coin, at the Treasury of the United States, or at the office of any assistant treasurer of the United States, and when so redeemed may be reissued; but no greater or less amount of such notes shall be outstanding at any time than the cost of the silver bullion and the standard silver dollars coined therefrom, then held in the Treasury purchased by such notes; and such Treasury notes shall be legal tender in payment of all debts, public and private, except where otherwise expressly stipulated in the contract, and shall be receivable for customs, taxes, and all public dues, and when so received may be reissued; and such notes, when held by any national banking association, may be counted as a part of its lawful reserve. That upon demand of the holder of any of the Treasury notes herein provided for the Secretary of the Treasury shall, under such regulations as he may prescribe, redeem such notes in gold or silver coin, at his discretion, it being the established policy of the United States to maintain the two metals on a parity with each other upon the present legal ratio, or such ratio as may be provided by law.

SEC. 3. That the Secretary of the Treasury shall each month coin two million ounces of the silver bullion purchased under the provisions of this act into standard silver dollars until the first day of July, eighteen hundred and ninety-one, and after that time he shall coin of the silver bullion purchased under the provisions of this act as much as may be necessary to provide for the redemption of the Treasury notes herein provided for, and any gain or seigniorage arising from such coinage shall be accounted for and paid into the Treasury.

SEC. 4. That the silver bullion purchased under the provisions of this act shall be subject to the requirements of existing law and the regulations of the mint service governing the methods of determining the amount of pure silver contained, and the amount of charges or deductions, if any, to be made.

SEC. 5. That so much of the act of February twenty-eight, eighteen hundred and seventy-eight, entitled "An act to authorize the coinage of the standard silver dollar and to restore its legal-tender character," as requires the monthly purchase and coinage of the same into silver dollars of not less than two million dollars, nor more than four million dollars' worth of silver bullion, is hereby repealed.

SEC. 6. That upon the passage of this act the balances standing with the Treasurer of the United States to the respective credits of national banks for deposits made to redeem the circulating notes of such banks, and all deposits thereafter receive for like purpose, shall be covered into the Treasury as a miscellaneous receipt, and the Treasurer of the United States shall redeem from the general cash in the Treasury the circulating notes of said banks which may come into his possession subject to redemption; and upon the certificate of the Comptroller of the Currency that such notes have been received by him and that they have been destroyed and that no new notes will be issued in their place, reimbursement of their amount shall be made to the Treasurer, under such regulations as the Secretary of the Treasury may prescribe, from an appropriation hereby, created, to be known, as National bank notes Redemption account: but the provisions of this act shall not apply to the deposits received under section three of the act of June twentieth, eighteen hundred and seventy-four, requiring every national bank to keep in lawful money with the Treasurer of the United States a sum equal to five percentum of its circulation, to be held and used for the redemption of its circulating notes; and the balance remaining of the deposits so covered shall, at the close of each month, be reported on the monthly public debt statement as debt of the United States bearing no interest."

"SEC. 7. That this act shall take effect thirty days from and after its passage."

Approved, July 14, 1890.

An effort was made in 1891 and two in 1892 to pass a bill for the free coinage of silver, but to no purpose.

The monetary policy of the United States since 1878 was now productive of its fatal results—the monetary crisis of 1892 and 1893, and from which the country is only now recovering. Early in 1893 it was clearly seen that the monthly purchase of 4,500,000 ounces of silver bullion had not and could not result in the maintenance of the price of that metal. There was a feeling of distrust abroad as to the stability of the currency of the United States, which not only discouraged investments in American securities, but encouraged their return.

From July 1, 1890, to June 30, 1893, the loss in gold by export was $188,000,000. On the 27th of June, 1893, India closed her mints to the free coinage of silver, which intensified the monetary crisis. Congress met in extraordinary session August 7, 1893, on the call of the President, to consider the monetary condition of the country, and on Novem-

MONETARY LEGISLATION. 105

ber 1, 1893, an act was passed repealing the purchasing clause of the act of 1890, after there had been bought under that act 168,764,682.53 ounces of fine silver, at a cost of $155,931,002.25. The act repealing the purchasing clause of the act of July 14, 1890, is as follows:

> That so much of the act approved July fourteenth, eighteen hundred and ninety, entitled "An act directing the purchase of silver bullion and issue of Treasury notes thereon, and for other purposes," as directs the Secretary of the Treasury to purchase from time to time silver bullion to the aggregate amount of four million five hundred thousand ounces, or so much thereof as may be offered in each month at the market price thereof, not exceeding one dollar for three hundred and seventy-one and twenty-five one-hundredths grains of pure silver, and to issue in payment for such purchases Treasury notes of the United States, be, and the same is hereby, repealed. And it is hereby declared to be the policy of the United States to continue the use of both gold and silver as standard money, and to coin both gold and silver into money of equal intrinsic and exchangeable value, such equality to be secured through international agreement, or by such safeguards of legislation as will insure the maintenance of the parity in value of the coins of the two metals, and the equal power of every dollar at all times in the markets and in the payment of debts. And it is hereby further declared that the efforts of the Government should be steadily directed to the establishment of such a safe system of bimetallism as will maintain at all times the equal power of every dollar coined or issued by the United States, in the markets and in the payment of debts.
> Approved, November 1, 1893.

The total amount of silver purchased under the acts of 1878 and 1890 was 459,946,701.09 fine ounces, at a cost of $464,210,262.92.

REFORM OF OUR CURRENCY SYSTEM.

From all that has been written above, it is clear that the result of the currency legislation of the United States, especially after 1873, has been to leave it a monetary system, as inconsistent, illogical, dangerous, and expensive as can well be imagined—one which inspires little confidence at home, and is certainly not conductive to our credit abroad. Its reform is one of the most important and most urgent political and financial questions of the hour, as well as one of the most difficult—full as difficult as the task that confronted Hamilton toward the close of the last century—on account of the magnitude, the diversity, and the conflict of interests, real or imaginary involved in its solution. But for this conflict of interests, sectional and other, and the erroneous ideas of the real principles of currency, to which a great portion of American voters have, for about thirty-three years, become habituated, the reform of our monetary system would not be so arduous, for the principles which should guide us in it are easily acquiesced in by an unbiased mind.

When laying the foundation of our monetary system embodied in the act of April 2, 1792, Hamilton said that such a system involved a great variety of considerations—intricate, nice, and important, What he then wrote of the proposed system may be profitably repeated to-day of the changes necessary in our present system in order to make it an agency of justice in the transactions of man with man, and a safeguard of the nation's credit in other lands. "The general state of debtor and creditor," says Hamilton, " all the relations and consequences of price, the essential interests of trade and industry, the value of all property, the whole income, both of the State and individuals, are liable to be sensibly influenced, beneficially or otherwise, by the judicious or injudicious regulation of this subject." And it is just as true now as it was in the days of Alexander Hamilton, that the "immense disorder which actually reigns in so delicate and important a concern, and the still greater disorder which is every moment possible, call loudly for reform."

When the experience of the United States from 1792 had shown that the maintenance of the double standard was an impossibility, Congress, hearkening to the teachings of history, adopted the gold standard by express provision. But after the adoption of the gold standard in 1873, the effect of all our subsequent currency legislation was a tendency to destroy that standard. This is especially true of the acts of February 28, 1878, and of July 14, 1890. Our currency legislation, since 1873, is but the reflection of the conflict of interests above referred to between the debtor and creditor classes, and between geographical sections of the country, resulting in an indefensible compromise between them. Considered as a whole, the laws relating to the currency since that year are lacking both in unity and continuity of purpose. They are not only inconsistent, contradictory, and obstructive of each other's operation, but are mutually destructive. Thus the act of February 12, 1873, provides that the one-dollar gold piece at the standard weight of 25.8 grains should be the unit of value, in other words, that the standard of the country should be gold monometallic. It dropped the standard silver dollar from the list of United States coins and provided that silver shall be legal tender only to the amount of $5. This act was plainly intended to make gold the sole metallic full legal-tender currency of the country as soon as specie payment could be resumed. But before that event the anticipated effect of the act of February 12, 1873, was in great part neutralized in 1878 by the passage, on February 28, of the act to authorize the coinage of the standard silver dollar and to restore its legal-tender character. True, this act did not authorize the free coinage of silver, but the obligation which it imposed on the Secretary of the Treasury to purchase, at the market price, silver bullion of not less than two million dollars' worth per month, and to cause the same to be coined as fast as purchased into standard silver dollars, had the same practical effect as free coinage, to this extent, that its tendency was to keep gold out of circulation; for, under that act, there was a total silver coinage of $378,168,793.

Another instance of the contradictory nature of our currency legislation is afforded by the act of January 14, 1875, authorizing the redemption of the legal-tender notes of the Government until the amount outstanding should be no more $300,000,000, and the act of May 31, 1878, requiring that, when such notes had been redeemed, they should not be canceled or retired, but should be again paid out and put in circulation—thus creating an endless chain of redemptions and reissues. To insure the redemption on presentation of the legal-tender notes, a gold reserve, which at the close of the fiscal year 1888 amounted to over $193,000,000, has had to be kept in the Treasury.

Since then, however, the gold reserve has shown a continual tendency to decline, and one of the principal financial difficulties which the Secretary of the Treasury has of late had to contend with has been its maintenance at a safe level. But before dwelling on the difficulty under our present currency legislation of maintaining a sufficient gold reserve it is necessary to refer briefly to the act of July 14, 1890, which intensified the evils produced by the act of February 12, 1878.

The act of July 14, 1890, directed to the Secretary of the Treasury to purchase, from time to time, silver bullion to the aggregate amount of 4,500,000 ounces, or so much thereof as might be offered each month at the market price thereof, not exceeding $1 for 371.25 grains of fine silver, and to issue, in payment of such purchases of silver bullion, Treasury notes of the United States. The act provided that these Treasury notes should be legal tender in payment of all debts, public and private, except where otherwise expressly stipulated in the contract. and should be receivable for customs, taxes, and all public dues; that when so received they might be reissued, and that upon demand of the holder, the Secretary of the Treasury should redeem them in gold or silver coin at his discretion, "it being the established policy of the United States to maintain the two metals at a parity with each other, upon the present legal ratio, or such ratio as may be provided by law." Under this act, the paper currency of the United States was increased $155,930,040. While, by its terms, it was left discretionary with the Secretary of the Treasury to redeem the notes issued under the act in gold or silver, the necessity of carrying out the policy of the United States to maintain gold and silver at par left him no option, when they were presented for redemption, except to give gold in exchange for them when demanded.

Not the least inconsistent and illogical feature of our inconsistent and illogical currency system is that, whereas the act of July 14, 1890, declares it to be the policy of the United States to keep gold and silver at par with each other, and the legal tender notes issued under the act therefore at par with gold, it provided the Secretary of the Treasury with no means adequate to that end.

On January 1, 1879, the date of the resumption of specie payments, the only currency except coin certificates which the Secretary of the Treasury was required to redeem in coin on presentation was the legal-tender notes, which then, as now, amounted to $346,681,016. The then Secretary was of the opinion that a gold reserve of $100,000,000 would be sufficient to maintain these $346,681,016 at par, and so long as there was no material increase in the amount of paper redeemable by the Government on presentation the reserve remained intact, and no serious disturbance occurred in the monetary system of the country. But an additional amount of Treasury notes of $155,930,940 were issued under the act of July 14, 1890, $141,092,280 of which are now (November 1, 1895) outstanding, making the direct Government obligations in use as money, $487,773,296. It is plain that $100,000,000 is not a sufficient sum in gold to insure the convertibility at all times of notes amounting to $487,773,-296, and to maintain them at par with gold.

But that heavy task is not the only one imposed on our gold reserve of $100,000,000. As under the laws of February 12, 1878, July 14, 1890, and March 3, 1891, $423,289,-309 in full legal-tender silver have been coined, against which $333,456,236 in certificates were outstanding November 1, 1895, and as the act of July 14, 1890, has declared it to be the established policy of the United States to maintain the two metals on a parity with each other, upon the present legal ratio or upon such ratio as may be provided by law, we have a total superstructure of $821,229,532 resting on the frail basis of a gold reserve of $100,000,000. Nothing is here said of the national-bank notes in circulation, now amounting to about $200,000,000, because they are redeemable on presentation at the banks themselves or at the Treasury in "lawful money" of the United States, and further because their ultimate redemption in gold coin is wholly satisfactory, the entire circulation of all the national banks being most amply secured by bonds of the United States. No worse commentary can be made on the expensive nature of our monetary system than that, to keep in repair this fragile foundation of $100,000,000, which is ever tending to disappear, it has been necessary within the past two years to borrow gold to the amount of $162,000,000, and this without adding to its firmness. Yet resort to the issue of bonds for this purpose, or repudiation, a silver basis for our circulating media, depreciation of the currency, and an impairment of all contracts, with all the evils attendant on silver monometallism were, under existing legal conditions, the only alternatives left to the Government.

The inconsistency of our currency legislation referred to above is faithfully described by the Secretary of the Treasury in his annual report of 1893;

> The unsatisfactory condition of our currency legislation has been for many years the cause of much discussion and disquietude among the people, and although one great disturbing element has been removed (by the repeal of the purchasing clause of the act of July 14, 1890), there still remain such inconsistencies in the laws and such differences between the forms and qualities of the various kinds of currency in use that private business is sometimes obstructed and the Treasury Department is constantly embarrassed in conducting the fiscal operations of the Government. There are now in circulation nine different kinds of currency, all except two being dependent directly or indirectly upon the credit of the United States. One statute requires the Secretary of the Treasury to redeem the old legal-tender notes in coin on presentation, and another compels him to reissue them, so that, no matter how often they are redeemed, they are never actually paid and extinguished. The act of July 14, 1890, provides that the Treasury notes issued in payment for silver bullion shall be redeemed in gold or

silver coin at the discretion of the Secretary, and when so redeemed may be reissued; but the same act also provides that no greater or less amonn tof such notes shall be outstanding at any time than the cost of the silver bullion and the standard silver dollars coined therefrom then held in the Treasury, purchased by such notes, and consequently when these notes are redeemed with silver coined from bullion purchased under the act, they can not be reissued, but must be retired and cancelled, for otherwise there would be a greater amount of notes outstanding than the cost of the bullion and coined dollars "then held in the Treasury."

And in his report for 1894 the Secretary points out the radical defects in our currency system in the following words:

I. The circulation of the United States notes as currency, and their current redemption in coin on demand.
II. The compulsory reissue of such notes after redemption.
III. The excessive accumulation and coinage of silver, and the issue of notes and certificates against it upon a ratio which greatly overvalues that metal as compared with the standard unit of value in this and other principal commercial countries.

It is plain that before the United States can have a reasonably safe currency these three radical defects must be remedied by appropriate legislation carried into practical effect.

The legal-tender notes definitively redeemed, and the Treasury notes issued under the act of July 14, 1890, out of the way, both having been exchanged dollar for dollar in gold, the currency of the United States would consist of gold and silver, of certificates of gold and silver which are merely certificates of deposit payable in gold or silver, as the case may be, on presentation, of national-bank notes, and currency certificates. The national-bank notes, although the guaranty of their ultimate redemption in gold coin is entirely satisfactory, are lacking in two of the essential elements of a bank-note currency. They are not redeemable in coin on presentation and can not be increased immediately in an emergency, no matter how large the metallic stock of the national banks—thus depriving the latter's circulation of elasticity. But, apart from these, after all the notes which the Government is pledged to maintain at par with gold had been cancelled, and when only gold and silver or their representatives remained in circulation, the United States would have the option of adopting the single gold standard and and limiting the legal-tender power of silver, as recommended by the Hon. John Sherman, Secretary of the Treasury, in his annual report for 1877, or of continuing the present system of the free coinage of gold with the suspension of the coinage of silver, and the limitation of the total amount of full legal-tender silver currency in such a way as not to expel gold from circulation or menace the country with the single silver standard.

The former alternative would be by far the most costly, and although doubtless in the end most satisfactory, no absolute necessity of resorting to it is as yet apparent. It would give the United States a monetary system akin to that of England. The latter alternative would leave it what is designated the "limping standard," and could be chosen at incomparably less cost than the former. It might, perhaps, be recommended as a suitable transition to the former, if the former should ever become imperative or easy of adoption. The experience of a great commercial country like France, and to some extent our own, has shown that where the coinage of full legal-tender silver is suspended, a very large amount of such silver can be maintained in circulation concurrently with gold and at par with it. France has a gold currency estimated at $850,000,000 and a silver full legal-tender currency of $430,000,000, and the silver exchangeable at par with gold. Whether the United States would be able to maintain the two metals at par under the second alternative without greatly reducing the amount of full legal-tender silver in circulation, either in the form of coin or of silver certificates, is a question which, in any serious endeavor to reform our currency, would have to receive careful consideration. In order that prices may, as in France, be expressed in terms of gold, there must be an abundance of gold, as compared with silver, in circulation. France has enough gold to meet all its engagements in that metal, and its large reserve of gold is the pledge of the full value of its silver coins. The 5-franc silver pieces of France circulate at par at home with gold, and lose abroad only a few *milles* per piece, corresponding to the cost of returning them to France. In France they can always be exchanged at par with gold. But even in France the French people keep no more 5-franc silver pieces in circulation than are necessary for the wants of trade. The remainder goes to the bank, and all endeavors made to lessen the silver reserve of that establishment and to increase the number of 5-franc silver pieces used in trade and by individuals have proved futile. The value of its silver full legal-tender coins has remained intact; but at the same time it has, like the value of paper not convertible on presentation, become a fiduciary value, and a part of the gold reserve is permanently withdrawn from circulation to guaranteee it. The mass of silver which is not capable of being utilized in exchange is not an element of wealth, or of strength, but an inconvenience and a drawback. So it would be in the United States even on the supposition that we were otherwise as favorably situated as France, for the maintenance, under our "limping standard," of the parity of gold and silver, by having relatively as large an amount of gold as that country and no greater demands upon it.

The increase of the amount of our gold currency, the continued supension of the coinage of full legal-tender silver, and even the lessening of the amount of such silver already in circulation, if that be necessary to keep it at par with gold, the final retirement of United States legal-tender notes and of the notes issued under the act of July 14, 1890, and the issuance, in lieu thereof, of gold coin, or of gold and silver coin, under proper limitation of the amount of the latter, seem to be the first steps requisite to endowing the United States with a currency which will inspire confidence at home and preserve the full credit of the nation abroad. Short of the single gold standard in the full meaning of the term, this is the least that a due regard for all interests and for the interests of all demands.

THE FREE COINAGE OF SILVER.

But, above all, it is certain that any scheme for the reform of our currency which does not contemplate the continued suspension of the coinage of full legal-tender silver, except by virtue of an international agreement, and, perhaps, at an altered ratio, would prove abortive. The free coinage of silver by the United States alone, especially at legal ratio of 1 : 16, while the commercial ratio is about 1 : 32, means for this country the single silver standard and depreciation of its currency, for at the legal ratio of 1 : 16 silver is not the equal of gold in coinage or out of it. This will become evident if, for the sake of argument, it be supposed that both metals are freely coined but both deprived of their legal-tender power.

If, in the battle of the standards, the legislative power did not interfere in favor of the depreciated metal, by making the coins stamped out of it full legal-tender, either alone or concurrently with the more valuable metal, the struggle for silver and the monetary question would soon be settled; and in the struggle for existence between the gold standard, the double standard and the silver standard, the fittest for all purposes of trade and in all forms of commercial intercourse would alone survive. It is safe to say that if in the United States at this moment the free and unlimited coinage of both gold and silver were guaranteed by law, but both gold and silver coins deprived of their legal-tender power, it being left to the creditor, whether a capitalist demanding the payment of interest on his loaned money or a day-laborer his week's wages, whether the millionaire receiving his dividends or collecting the value of his coupons, the planter the price of his cotton or tobacco, the farmer of his wheat, or the humble shop-keeper that of the few yards of cloth, or the few pounds of beef or butter he has sold, all would demand the coin least liable to fluctuation of value and farthest removed from the reach of unforseen contingencies—that is, the millionaire and laborer, the rich and the poor man alike would insist on payment in gold, and would refuse it in silver.

During the last generation—that is, ever since the 25th of February, 1862, when the Government of the United States made its paper evidences of indebtedness legal tender—many have naturally grown up with all sorts of misconceptions and delusions on the important subject of the currency. Hence it is that their fundamental notion of money is a false one, and although they know full well that the silver coins of the United States at present owe nearly half their value to the stamp of the mint which they bear and the pledge of the Government to maintain them at par with gold, and that, to that extent, the value of these silver coins is fictitious and not real, they persist in preferring shadow to substance in the currency of the country, or at least to consider shadow quite as good as substance. Although aware that 1,000 silver dollars bearing the stamp of a United States mint, thrown into the melting pot and reduced to the form of bullion, will produce a quantity of metal that will yield the holder little more than $500 in any market of the world, while 1,000 gold dollars also bearing the stamp of the United States, subjected to the same process, will come out of the crucible still worth $1,000 in any country of the world, they insist that the silver and the gold are equally good currency.

They have apparently never asked themselves what becomes of nearly 50 per cent. of the value of the silver dollar after the stamp of the United States mint has been obliterated from it and it has been changed in shape; in what the departed value consisted while the stamp remained intact and the form of the coin unaltered; whether the lost value was real or imaginary; whether the stamp was the expression of a truth or the contrary; and whether, without the whole power of the courts and of the executive back of it, the silver dollar would pass on its own intrinsic merits, or otherwise than by the compulsory circulation given it by the strong hand of the law. If, indeed, the law favored neither a gold currency above a silver currency, nor a silver currency above a gold, but left it to the free and unconstrained action of the citizens to choose between them, they would invariably choose that which was always and everywhere least subject to deterioration, whose value depended upon itself and not upon Congress, nor upon legal-tender acts, but upon free and not compulsory acceptance; that is, under the circumstances of the present time, they would choose gold and not silver.

One infallible test and measure of the soundness of a metallic or other currency is to be found in the answer to the question, whether deprived of the legal-tender power guaranteed it by the State it would still be sought after and voluntarily received in payment at its full nominal value. If it should, then it is plain that it is received because of some quality inherent in itself, something which the law does not endow it with and can not take from it. If it would not, then it is just as plain that it is accepted under compulsion, and that but for the coercive power of the State forcing the creditor to receive it, it would not circulate at its full nominal value. Tested in this way, it would not be long before even the owners of silver would cease advocating its use as money equally with gold and bringing it to the mints to be coined into a currency which no one was willing to receive and which would therefore remain on their hands as useless, except for employment in the arts, as if it had never been extracted from the mines. In short, in obedience to the natural law of the survival of the fittest, in the struggle of the standards for existence, the gold standard would prevail and the better money drive out the worse, for Gresham's law does not operate where the State does not make the worse money legal-tender, and compel the creditor to receive it even when his self-interest would induce him to choose the better. All highly civilized countries and all great commercial nations, with the exception of the United States, have, for reasons of this nature, pronounced in favor of the gold standard for the Latin Union may be said to have the gold standard *de facto*. The monetary history of the world, especially since 1871, may be cited as evidence of this fact.

"OUR CURRENCY SYSTEM."

SPEECH DELIVERED BY

HON. JAMES H. ECKELS,
Comptroller of the Currency,

AT THE ANNUAL DINNER OF THE

CHICAGO REAL ESTATE BOARD.

CHICAGO, ILL.

HELD AT

THE AUDITORIUM HOTEL,

Thursday Evening, January 16, 1896.

I accepted the invitation to be present upon this occasion and speak on the subject "Our Currency System" largely because of my knowledge of the interest taken by this organization in every question of public moment. It is, I believe, a boast of the Chicago Real Estate Board that at no time in its history have its members failed in their earnest support of any measure or cause which promised good to the citizen. If as yet it has not wrought all the reforms hoped for, still it has completely accomplished some and created a public sentiment which ultimately must accomplish all. It has, I am confident, been a means of direct saving to every tax payer of this city and an efficient instrumentality in more perfectly protecting him in his constitutionally guaranteed "right of property." If it but persists in its announced determination to maintain a watchful guardianship over the acts of those here entrusted with public power and insists upon a betterment in legislation affecting the great interests with which its members have to do, the day is not far distant when the people of Illinois will have property assessments which are fairly and equitably made, rates of taxation that are not unnecessarily and exorbitantly high, a code of revenue laws resting upon a just and scientific basis and a standard of excellency and honesty established among those who enforced them that will give rise to no fear of blackmail upon the one hand or of favoritism on the other.

But these are matters for others to discuss. I leave them in order to direct your attention to a question of wider scope than any one or all of them and of an importance greater in its immediate bearing upon your own well being than even the manner in which your assessments are made, the rate of taxation levied upon your lands or the method of making up the titles thereto. I do not exaggerate when I say that the most momentous question presented to each here present is the Currency question. It is one neither of politics nor of political preferment. It is, as you more than all others ought to realize, one of business self preservation, and as such should command at the hands of those who are sworn to guard and preserve the people's rights a statesmanship and patriotism commensurate with the magnitude of the interests involved. It ought, as well, to enlist a public sentiment that should bring a swift punishment upon those who would make it the plaything of party desires and the subject of mere political oratory.

One of the worlds most distinguished philosophic historians, has said that "the indispensible thing for a politician is a knowledge of political economy and history." If the statement be correct a review of the currency legislation of this country for a third of a century demonstrates that few if any politicians in the historian sense have had to do with it. In all the range of it evidence is everywhere to be had of a disregard of the underlying principles of political economy, and a woeful ignorance of the facts of monetary history. An analysis of its parts bears testimony to the truths of the assertion. A consideration of the whole places it beyond cavil. That which we term "our currency system" is one in name only. It lacks every element of that which rightfully should be called a system. It violates in every essential feature that which in all other departments of Governmental affairs we denominate a system. It is not an orderly combination of parts into a whole according to some rational principle or organic idea. Throughout all of it there is want of unity, and instead of its presenting to the world financial completeness it exhibits itself as a work of "shreds and patches."

I am not unmindful that some of the evils of it found their origin in the flush and excitement of a great war, when men yielded their better judgment to what seemed the demands of patriotism, and sanctioned currency legislation that under other and different circumstances, they would never have consented should find place upon the statute book. But the era of war long ago passed away, and since that day through three decades of peace, legislative bodies of varying political faith have convened at the Nation's Capitol, and yet our currency laws are still inharmonious, productive of loss to every citizen and a cause of continuing anxiety to the Nation's executive officers. We have had legislation, some of it bearing promise of working out the country's financial salvation, but in every such instance it has been changed and amended into that which has made it an engine for harm. The citizen who studies the ways of governments and enquires into the operations of financial laws, might tolerate during the war period, with some degree of patience, as did the son of the great financier Albert Gallatin, the sobriquet of "an odd fish" as applied to him by a member of Congress in 1862, when he opposed the doctrine of currency fiatism, but thirty years after its close they have right to complain when currency fiatism in silver and paper issues of the government are still sanctioned by legislative enact-enactment. Nowhere in any nation whether of great or little power is there to be found a currency and financial system so inadequate for the purposes to be accomplished as that of the United States. It presents in its circulation feature the singular spectacle of nine different kinds of currency, all except two being directly or indirectly dependent upon the credit of the United States. The treasury department established by it is the greatest banking institution in the land clothed with the least powers for its self-preservation and beneficial action. One statute requires the Secretary of the Treasury to redeem the legal-tender notes in coin on presentation and another compels him to pay them out that they may return again and again for redemption. Upon every hand it is an embarrassment to the proper conduct of the business affairs of the country. It adds to their embarassments by the forced inflation of the volume of the circulating medium at one time and the forced contraction through the operation of the Sub-treasury system at another. Designing to have the banks created under it and subject to governmental supervision supply the currency needs of the country, it still insists on competing with them in their note issuing function, and prevents through tax and other barriers which it erects, their attaining the very end for which they were brought into being.

By the operation of the Bland-Allison Act it brought about the coining of many millions of silver dollars at a value far more than the commercial value of the silver metal in them, and of far less value than the metal in the gold dollar with which it provides they shall be of equal legal-tender value, and along side of which they are expected to circulate. And as if to add the crowning act to a series of complications already perplexing to an unheard of degree, the Sherman Act has given to us still other silver dollars and notes to burden an already overburdened gold reserve, without in the smallest measure adding to its safe guards.

We search in vain to find some solid foundation upon which all this structure rests, but the statute books reveal nothing, save that there is drawn about all these what is deemed the sacred circle of its protection, in the declaration ostentatiously made, that it is "the established policy of the United States to maintain the two metals at a parity with each other upon the present legal ratio or such ratio as may be provided by law." It makes the declaration, and then to proclaim the sham and pretense of it, denies to the Secretary of the Treasury such full and adequate powers as would enable him, under any and all circumstances, to enforce that policy to the credit of the Nation and with the least expense to the citizen.

In the contemplation of such a series of contradictions and inconsistencies the business men of this Nation may well decry currency conditions so unwholesome, and demand a speedy remedying of them at the hands of the law-making power. No stronger evidence could be had that the whole system is radically wrong and weakening to our financial world, than the fact that here and everywhere, as it now stands, it is the one great subject of discussion and debate. No one is arguing as to the foundation of our form of government, because all recognize the inherent correctness of the principles upon which it rests. Our system of jurisprudence is beyond question, and neither in legislative hall nor in the columns of the press is it assailed. But the private citizen in business, the National legislator and executive officers of the government are all confessing by their daily acts and conversation that this one first essential to a people's prosperity is with us, so far from being sound, as to be absolutely weak and dangerous.

I will not within the space of time allotted to the making of this response undertake to discuss more than one element in this system, which by reason of the dangers attendant upon it stands forth conspicuously above all the rest—the greenback element. I cite it because the harm which it is doing must be manifest to all; because every bond issue made to preserve the gold reserve in the treasury bears testimony to the expense of it to the tax payer and every measure introduced in Congress to cancel the indebtedness which it represents, or prevent the too great rapidity and repetition of the presenting of it for redemption, proclaims its harmfulness. It would be foolish to undertake to conceal that the source of our difficulty lies in the fear that the United States cannot in the face of existing laws maintain the gold standard as its unit of value. The faintest suspicion that it will not now or in the future meet its obligations in conformity with that fine sense of financial integrity which has heretofore been observed, gives the business world such a shock that we witness on every hand a cessation of new undertakings and a constant query as to our future. There is no relief for this situation in the great individual wealth of our individual citizens nor in their individual desire to maintain their credit. The unlimited resources of the country and the unbounded energies of the people are in and of themselves equally unavailing in giving aid and comfort. The fault lies in the Government's financial system and not in the rule of conduct which guides each individual as an individual. Until the national fault is eradicated, the individual must continue to suffer for his country's folly both in purse and in reputation. Those abroad who deal with us take their estimate of our individual financial integrity by that of our government. They do not rank the individual American's honesty higher than his government's honesty and they will not believe him willing to pay his contracts in gold, if his government substitutes therefore paper or a discredited metal, giving in real value but a portion of its purport value and the balance in governmental fiat.

Every law placed upon the statute books, therefore which tends to make at any time the Government's credit the least in doubt must injuriously affect every business relation, and work loss to every citizen. Equally effective as a cause of weakness and distrust must be the continual suggestion of laws which would substitute a debased standard of value for the one in vogue, and not less harmful than either the former or the latter evil is the failure to repeal statutes that confessedly are a source of loss. The observant citizen who notes the effect of events must see that the greatest danger to-day to every business interest, and the cause of so much stagnation in bank, factory, shop and store is the legal tender issue, and compulsory reissue by the Government. They are condemned by the student of finance familiar with the world's monetary history and with equal emphasis by the man of affairs trained in the school of business affairs. In their effect and operation they to-day constitute the strongest hope of the advocates of the free coinage of silver, thus working a double hindrance to the return of complete prosperity. The advocate of the free coinage of silver believes that through them a silver basis must ultimately be reached and because of this they resist their payment and cancellation unless silver dollars at the ratio of sixteen to one be substituted in their stead. The daily question whether the government can maintain a gold reserve adequate to meet these demand obligations as they are presented; the anxiety arising from the fear of a "gold run" upon the Treasury; the necessity of resorting to a cumbersome statute in order to issue coin bonds to maintain the parity of the metals; the frequency of such issues—all, coupled with the avowed hope of many free silver legislators of breaking down the government's gold credit and reaching a silver basis, are working incalculable injury.

The legal tender issues of the Government ought and must be redeemed and retired, if the American people are to be rid of the recurring danger and loss arising from their being a part of our currency issues. The people should look back upon the history of their creation and study the effect which they have had upon their welfare. Their character and their history seem now to be little considered. They are demand obligations never retired, fixed as to volume, and from their inception a source of loss and expense to the people. They doubled the cost of the civil war and prematurely drove us from a specie basis to one, for many years, of irredeemable paper. At the time they were first sent forth their most ardent advocate apologized for their issue and promised quick payment of them. As an earnest of this they were at the time made convertible into an interest bearing bond. Had it not been for the circumstances surrounding the government not a dozen votes could have been obtained in either the Senate of the House for the legal tender principle. Secretary Chase was dragooned only through what he mistakably believed to be dire necessity into giving his official sanction to them. He repudiated them when as Chief Justice of the Supreme Court of the United States he gave a legal decision covering the principle upon which they rest, He flatly declined to advocate them in his report to Congress. It was stated and uncontradicted at the time that prior to the Act of 1862 not only was such a law never passed, but such a law was never voted on, never proposed, never introduced, never recommended by any department of the Government and that such a measure was never seriously entertained in debate in either branch of Congress. The present senior Senator from Vermont, Mr. Justin S. Morrill, then a member of the committee of Ways and Means of the House, in an extremely able speech characterized them as "the precursor of a prolific brood of promises" and the bill as "a measure not blessed by one sound precedent and damned by all." His prediction of thirty-four years ago and his characterization of them have been fully justified by the series of events which have marked our history since that time and to-day as he recurs to the words then spoken, he must take melancholy satisfaction in the knowledge that his statesmenship unlike that of some others that day was sufficient to see beyond the pressing demand of a single hour of the nation's life. The temporary issues of that day despite the appeals of Chief Executives and Secretaries of the Treasury, are yet a part of the fixed volume of our currency. From first to last they have been the greatest burden and most expensive debt ever placed upon the Government. The loss to the people through speculation engendered by them, the financial heresies to which they have given birth, the damage to individual business enterprise and credit through the recurring doubt as to the ability of the Government to maintain the payment of them in gold cannot be reckoned in figures. But every panic we have had, and every stagnation in business which has come upon us mark their distinctive influence.

It is asserted that when the revenues of the Government exceed the necessary expenditures bond issues will cease, and no further trouble follow. The difficulty, however, goes beyond the question of revenue and touches the vital point in trenching upon the confidence of those dealing with us in our ability to always pay these obligations in gold. Complete confidence cannot be restored by simply increasing the governmental income; but even if it could there would be no guarantee against future impairment of it through the same cause. There is but one road to absolute safety, and that lies through their payment and cancellation. When that end is accomplished we will have done much to rid the people of the belief now entertained, that in the fiat of the Government is some magic power which from nothing can bring forth something of intrinsic value.

I am aware that all this cannot be brought about without a struggle. It rests with the nation's law making powers to say whether the people shall be freed from this "body of death" which bears upon them or whether they shall continue to carry it. From those who stand within the innei circle of legislative action the announcement comes that nothing can be done unless concessions are made to interests the harmful results of which no man can foretell. If such be the truth the duty is placed upon every man who has his country's interests at heart and would put an end to the losses now entailed upon himself and neighbor to raise his voice in protest against either inaction or concession. With the American people the most potent force for good is the might of public opinion. Against the power of it when once aroused no legislator has ever yet been able to stand no matter how loud his boastful threats or arrogant his demeanor. Enforced by it the President of the United States wrung from unwilling and hostile legislators the repeal of a statute that was defended through weeks by those who proclaimed that their never could be with them either compromise or surrender. It did erase the Sherman silver purchasing act. It will accomplish no less to-day for the welfare of the citizen if it is again as earnestly appealed to.

www.ingramcontent.com/pod-product-compliance
Lightning Source LLC
Chambersburg PA
CBHW022137160426

43197CB00009B/1332